# AMERICAN SPITFIRE
## CAMOUFLAGE & MARKINGS

*By..*
# Paul Ludwig and Malcolm Laird

- Illustrated by Malcolm Laird -

*The first Spitfire ever to wear USAAF markings..*

Two Officers of Brigadier General Frank Hunter's staff, in England 1942, with the first Spitfire to wear USAAF markings. Left, unidentified, right J. Francis Taylor. The picture  was taken by Colonel Cass Hough, also a member of Hunter's staff.

No. 3 in the Classic Warbirds series

" 'American Spitfire – Camouflage and Markings' is the third book in Ventura's Classic Warbird series.
*-At least one further part will cover other USAAF Spitfire Groups.-*

Both Paul Ludwig and myself thank Mrs Pat Keen, author of the authoritative 'Eyes of the Eighth' about the 7th Photo Reconnaissance Group, for putting us in touch. She recommended Paul as a researcher on USAAF Spitfire Groups and we decided to develop our ideas based around Paul's photo collection and historical research, and my colour illustrations and knowledge of their camouflage and markings.

Paul Ludwig, on the left and Malcolm Laird

Paul Ludwig served as a US Navy pilot from 1954 to 1958. After gaining his wings in 1955 he was commissioned and flew the Douglas AD-6 Skyraider with VA-145 on a tour in the Western Pacific aboard the U.S.S. Hornet in 1957. He was an instructor on Skyraiders in 1957 and 1958 but returned to civilian life later that year and joined Northwest Airlines. He retired as a 747 Captain after 36 years of airline flying, having logged 23,000 hours. Paul, who lives in Seattle, Washington began his research into aviation subjects in 1980 and plans to publish a major work on the development of fighter escort doctrine in the USAAF, in the future.

My thanks to David Frowen, whose editing and proof reading was most appreciated. Also, thanks to Rex Barker and Jim Dietz for their generous assistance."

*Malcolm Laird*

"My initial interest in USAAF Spitfires came when I sat down for a beer with the late Lt. John Fawcett, who lived here in Seattle with his wife 'Lady Ellen' (see page 54). John's help and encouragement with my research turned out to be invaluable. At 31st FG reunions I received great friendship and assistance from Col. Frank Hill, Capt. Harry Barr, Lt. Bill Skinner, Brig. Gen. Harrison Thyng and Maj. Gen. C.M. McCorkle. Long weeks of research at the National Archives in Washington, D.C. and at the Simpson Historical Research Library at Maxwell AFB in Alabama, were aided by the extremely helpful staff there.
My lovely wife JoAnne has given me daily support for my idea to write this brief history.
Also, thanks again to Malcolm Laird and all those supporters I may not have mentioned individually."

*Paul Ludwig*

## FRONT COVER COLOUR ILLUSTRATIONS..

- Spitfire Mk Vʙ 'MX-R' of the 307th FS, England, July/August 1942
- Spitfire Mk Vᴄ (trop) of the 307th FS, North Africa, 1943
- Captain Harry Barr's Spitfire Mk IX of the 309th FS, Italy, December 1943
- Lieutenant John Fawcett's Spitfire Mk IX of the 309th FS, Italy, March 1944
- Background collage, two photos of 307th FS pilots in North Africa.

Classic Warbirds series No 3 -
American Spitfire - Camouflage & Markings
**Authors..** Paul Ludwig & Malcolm Laird
**Colour Illustrations..** Malcolm Laird
**Layout & design..** Judy Laird

**Published by Ventura Publications**
P.O. Box 10-213,
Wellington,
New Zealand
**Phone +64(4)384 3040 Fax +64(4)385 8189**
**E-mail malcolm.laird@waug.actrix.gen.nz**

ISBN 0-9583594-3-1 © Copyright 1998. First Impression 1998

# INTRODUCTION

The reasons why some USAAF Fighter Groups based in Europe were equipped with British Spitfires for two years are, in essence, quite straight forward. In July 1942 the Spitfire's excellent combat performance was needed. However it's short range was always a problem and, by late 1943 with the P-51B Mustang available, the Spitfire's short range could no longer be tolerated and so the business-like Mustang replaced the elegant Spitfire.

Camouflage and markings worn by USAAF Spitfires followed the simple formula of RAF camouflage and USAAF markings. Cocarde and code letter size, style and placement varied greatly, because markings were applied at unit level and new aircraft were always received still wearing RAF roundels. Add to this, squadron badges and a myriad of personal markings and you have some of the most colourful Spitfires of the Second World War. Variations were many in terms of markings but few in terms of camouflage – except for field repainted aircraft and the various Spitfire 'hacks' retained by squadrons after the transition to Mustangs in April 1944.

# CONTENTS

# RANGE EXTENSION PROGRAM

One of the most difficult aircraft development problems during the Second World War was to provide a single-engine, long-range, escort fighter.

Lord Portal, Chief of Air-Staff, RAF, since October 1940; refused to allow development effort diverted from other pressing projects to develop a long-range Supermarine Spitfire fighter variant, even though by October 1942 PR.Mk XI reconnaissance planes were in production. These could fly to Berlin and back (admittedly with no fuel allowance for combat) more than a year before the first North American P-51B Mustang arrived in the European Theatre of Operations (ETO).

Spitfire Mk IX MK210 at Wright Field in early 1944. It wears a factory applied RAF Temperate Land Scheme of *Dark Green* and *Ocean Grey* upper surfaces with *Medium Sea Grey* lower surfaces, *Sky* spinner and 18" rear fuselage band. Note the fuel filler cap, for the extra fuselage tank, below the radio mast. (USAAF)

Prior to January 1944 the USAAF preferred the Lockheed P-38 Lightning as a long-range fighter, with the P-51 seen merely as a fighter bomber. However, work by the USAAF 'Fighter Airplane Range Extension Program' from September 1943, and the realisation that the magnificent P-51B possessed the longest range of any fighter in the world, saved the Eighth Air Force (8th AF) daylight bombing campaign over Europe. The 15th AF, in Italy, also needed the P-51B in order to reach the Nazi heartland.

General H H 'Hap' Arnold, Chief of the USAAF, decided to 'tweak the noses' of the RAF for not attempting to develop the Spitfire into a long-range fighter. He obtained two Spitfire Mk IX's, including MK210, and had engineers at Wright Field, Ohio, convert every available interior space into fuel tanks and add under-wing drop tanks. Fulfilling General Arnold's plan, two Wright Field test pilots were to fly the Spitfires

Spitfire Mk IX MK210, fitted with extra fuel tanks, including P-51 style drop tanks. Note the lack of yellow leading edge strip, standard on RAF Fighter Command aircraft. (USAAF)

nonstop across the Atlantic and thereby demonstrate to the RAF the Spitfire's range potential.

Departing in May 1944, Lt. Colonel Gustav Lundquist – Chief Experimental Fighter Test Pilot of the Flight Test Section, Wright Field – flew MK210 to Boscombe Down, England, together with the second modified Spitfire and a B-25 which acted as their navigational pathfinder. Refuelling stops were to be made at Goose Bay, Baffin Island, Bluie West 8 in Greenland, Iceland and Prestwick in Scotland. Leaving Wright Field, the second Spitfire experienced engine problems and Lundquist waited for it in Greenland. The three aircraft eventually flew on to England in June, demonstrating that a truly long-range Spitfire fighter was possible.

The Spitfire is sometimes referred to as merely a 'point defence interceptor' when compared unfavourably to the Mustang. Supporters of the Mustang conveniently forget that in 1943 the Republic P-47 Thunderbolt, which was the USAAF's main fighter in Europe at that time, had a radius of action little greater than the Spitfire – until it was fitted with drop-tanks. In any case, the British never took up this American initiative. Possibly the complex Spitfire wing would need to be completely re-stressed/re-engineered for it to carry the extra weight of fuel under combat conditions. Maintaining production took precedence.

Lt. Colonel (later Brigadier General) Gustav Lundquist with Spitfire Mk IX MK210 at Bluie West 8, Greenland, where his flight to England was delayed while he waited for the second Spitfire which was to accompany him to England. In Greenland Sergeant Petta added this outrageous nose art to MK210. Tolly was Lundquist's wife's name and one can only assume that the lady is on the telephone giving the RAF a 'wake-up-call' about the Spitfires range potential. (Gen. G Lundquist)

A Lockheed P-38F Lightning and Spitfire Mk VA at Lockheed Air Terminal, Burbank, California. Colonel Ben Kelsey had just flown the Spitfire from Wright Field. The 8th AF could have used P-38s as escort fighters in the ETO much earlier than it did. Priority for the type was passed to the Pacific Theatre where P-38s were employed with great success, using their speed and fire-power against more manoeuvrable Japanese opponents. (B Kelsey, NASM)

# SPITFIRES FOR THE 31ST FIGHTER GROUP

Several units of the United States Army Air Forces (USAAF) operated the Supermarine Spitfire during the Second World War, with the 31st Fighter Group (31st FG) being the most well known. The others were the 52nd FG, the 4th FG (for a six month period), a squadron of the 7th Photo Reconnaissance Group and some smaller units. After 1942 the USAAF gave little publicity to its units operating foreign built equipment, so the 31st FG was never accorded much fame back in the US, until it converted to the North American P-51B Mustang, in April 1944. By that time the USAAF needed to use it's fighters as long-range escorts – a role the Spitfire could not fulfil.

Members of the 40th PS in front of one of their Curtiss P-40 Tomahawks. From the left are Lt. Zins, Lt. Elliot, Capt. A P Clark – Commanding Officer, a Curtiss representative, Lt. S M Smith, Lt. Frank Hill, Lt. McGary, Unknown. Clark remained with the Group when its new squadrons, the 307th, 308th and 309th were created. He was later shot down during the Dieppe debacle and captured by the Germans. Post war he rose to the rank of Lieutenant General. (General Clark)

The small United States Army Air Corps had been under severe financial constraints throughout the 'Great Depression' of the 1930s. Within the USAAC, the development of fighter aircraft took a back seat to the promotion of the four-engine strategic bomber – which appeared in the form of the famous B-17 Flying Fortress. The Army, with its view that it's Air Corps was just airborne artillery, truly stunted the development of modern monoplane fighters in the years leading up to the Second World War. Fortunately many officers in the Air Corps identified the mission of the bomber as strategic in nature and not merely flying artillery. During this period of behind-the-scenes argument emphasis on fighter development, particularly as regards to range, was minimal.

When Germany invaded Poland in September 1939, France, Great Britain and their allies declared war on Germany. The writing was on the wall that the United States would eventually be dragged into this

A man destined to fight with distinction in three wars. 1st Lieutenant Harrison Thyng at New Orleans in 1942, with the 31st PG's new P-40B Tomahawks. Thyng was a WWII Ace flying piston engined fighters and an Ace on jet fighters in Korea. Later still he flew in the Vietnam War.

Note the early-war style cocarde with the red centre dot. This style of national marking was introduced in 1921 and was only replaced in May 1942, for the benefit of American aircraft operating against the Japanese. The change was to eliminate any confusion with the Japanese 'meatball' insignia. (Groseclose)

European conflict just as it had in 1917. President Franklin Roosevelt opened the nation's purse strings to modernise and expand the Army and Navy. Many minds realised the importance of a strong Air Force and, only months after the war in Europe began, Major General Arnold, Chief of the United States Army Air Corps, began the task of upgrading his forces. His aim was equality or superiority with the larger German, Japanese and British air forces who then operated the most advanced fighter types.

## FORMATION OF THE 31ST PG

Prior to 1942 all American fighter groups were known as Pursuit Groups (PG) and for a time Head Quarters Air Force (HQAF) had only one Pursuit Group, the 1st PG. New National Defence Acts promulgated the 31st PG – among others – which split from the 1st PG in February 1940. The new Group was based at Selfridge Field northeast of Detroit, Michigan, 'Home of the Pursuit Groups'. At the time of it's formation, the 31st PG consisted of a Headquarters squadron plus the 39th, 40th and 41st PS (Pursuit Squadrons), all commanded by Colonel Harold H George.

The 31st PG was given high priority to receive the most modern American fighters. However, with the Bell P-39 and Curtiss P-40 just commencing production, the 31st operated obsolete P-26s, P-35s and various other cast-offs until these new fighter types became available. The Group received P-39s in mid-1941 and began working up alongside the 52nd PG in northern Michigan (The 52nd was also destined to operate the Spitfire for two years and the two Groups enjoyed a long and friendly rivalry).

## TRAINING

The 31st PG operated from several bases in the southeastern United States before settling at Baer Field near Fort Wayne, Indiana, in December 1941. When the Japanese attacked Pearl Harbour on 7 December 1941, the Nation declared war on Japan and Germany. The 31st PG was ordered to Paine Field , north of Seattle, Washington, in anticipation of Japanese attacks on the west coast of the United States. Expansion of the USAAC now reached fever pitch, with the 31st PG as one of it's senior units.

A 307th FS Spitfire Mk VB, EN799, taxis for take-off at Manston, England, late July or August 1942.

This aircraft, with its serial in very small letters on the upper fin, is a good example of the first Spitfires received and re-marked by the 31st FG. The fuselage and fin areas where the old RAF markings have been completely over-painted with fresh *Ocean Grey,* are clearly discernable. The new cocardes are 40" on the upper wing and 30" on the fuselage and lower wing, *Sky* codes are 24" high. Note the 307th FS badge under the cockpit. (via B Anderson)

New Pursuit Groups were quickly formed by taking some trained men from the 1st and 31st to form the nucleus of new groups. For the 31st the consequence of this was that its administrative organisation and cadre of experienced pilots stayed on the west coast; but the Group lost its three squadrons to the newly formed 35th PG which was posted to the South West Pacific to fight the Japanese. In February 1942, what remained of the 31st PG was sent to New Orleans where, equipped with some P-40s, the group was brought up to full strength again. Colonel George was replaced by Colonel John R. Hawkins and the cadres of the old

39th, 40th, & 41st squadrons formed three new squadrons, the 307th, 308th and 309th, commanded by Lieutenants Marvin McNickle, Fred Dean and Harrison Thyng respectively.

Rapid progress was achieved in bringing the Group up to strength and, by the end of January 1942, it was equipped with Bell P-39 Airacobras and training hard at New Orleans.

In mid-1941 the Army Air Corps had been renamed the United States Army Air Forces. In May 1942 Pursuit Groups were renamed Fighter Groups (FG) and Pursuit Squadrons became Fighter Squadrons (FS). The 31st FG was assigned to the new 8th AF, which became America's greatest air armada.

Lieutenant Harrison Thyng in standard RAF flying gear posing on an RAF-marked Spitfire, probably at the time the 31st FG collected its first Spitfires. This photo illustrates the early style external armoured windscreen, non-streamlined rear-view mirror and flat sided canopy. (H Thyng)

**Below**. Pilots of 'B' Flight, 308th FS, Westhampnett RAF Station, September 1942. From the left are, Charles Van Reed, Mathew Mosby, Adrian A Davis, E G Johnson, Derwood Smith, Westley Ballard, John Ramer and Frank Hill. Note the battery starter cart required to start a Spitfire Mk V. (F Hill)

## FERRY FLIGHT PLANS

In 1942 when the 8th AF was created specifically to serve in England, a plan was hatched to fly *all* its aircraft to England. This included having the 31st fly its P-39s across the cold, foreboding North Atlantic Ocean, with fuel stops along the way, formatting on B-17 Flying Fortress 'pathfinders' for navigation. Weather along this route was frequently terrible, the pilot's over-water navigation was rudimentary (should they become separated from the B-17) and blind-flying experience was nonexistent. The USAAF believed that the P-39 was adequate to fight the Luftwaffe and considerable effort was wasted in trialing methods to fly the P-39s to England. One minor reason given for even considering ferrying the P-39s was an acute shortage of ships to transport aircraft as deck cargo – a practice which later become commonplace.

Several versions of history exist as to why the P-39s were finally abandoned and the two American Groups equipped with Spitfires. One is that the pathfinder B-17s, based at Grenier Field, could not be spared to accompany the 31st FG and were diverted to fight a Japanese invasion in the North Pacific Aleutian Island chain. In any case, the 31st and 52nd FGs did practice formation flying with some B-17s at Grenier Field, but found this most difficult while equipped with the huge 175 gallon belly tanks needed to fly the longest over-water legs connecting the USA, Canada, Greenland, Iceland and Northern Ireland. Still, the USAAF persisted with the ferry plan and ordered the 52nd FG to continue practising formation flying with B-17s, even in bad weather. Two pilots from the Group spun-out, crashed and were killed during practice. Fortunately for the remaining pilots, the plan was eventually abandoned.

Another factor in the Spitfire's favour was that, while Lend-Lease was primarily a mechanism for America to equip Britain with armaments, the Spitfires provided some measure of equipment flow in the other direction, to balance-the-books. However, perhaps the most compelling

1st Lieutenant James M Ingham of the 309th FS in his Spitfire Mk VB at Kenley, England, July 1942. This aircraft is painted in the standard RAF Temperate Land Scheme of *Dark Green* and *Ocean Grey* upper surfaces with *Medium Sea Grey* lower surfaces. The spinner and 18" rear fuselage bands are *sky* and wing leading edge strip starting outboard of the cannons is *Ident. Yellow*.

Note Ingham's personal Star of David marking, the 'shadow' of the old RAF under-wing roundel and the interesting method of taping over the cannon barrels. (J Ingham)

Spitfire Mk VB 'MX-D' EN851 flown by Lt. R Wooten with the 307th FS at Merston, West Sussex, July/August 1942. This aircraft still carries it's RAF presentation name 'Lima Challenger' on both sides of the nose. Note the fresh *Ocean Grey* paint used to obliterate the RAF roundel and fin flash and the 30' fuselage cocarde. (B Anderson)

reason was simply that the USAAF was finally convinced, from European combat reports, that the P-39 simply would not have survived in the air battles already raging over Europe.

History records that the 31st FG departed for England on 3 June 1942 while the 52nd FG left in July and August. Both Groups were now to be equipped with Supermarine Spitfires – already a very famous fighter having captured the public imagination during the Battle of Britain.

## ENGLAND – INTO ACTION

In May 1942, in preparation for transfer overseas, the 31st FG was split into air and ground echelons. The Ground Echelon was put on a train for Fort Dix, New Jersey, then embarked ship for Scotland, arriving

A Spitfire Mk VB of the 308th FS sits on the grass at Tangmere, October 1942. This aircraft wears the standard RAF Temperate Land Scheme and its fuselage cocarde has the yellow ring 8th AF aircraft were ordered to carry from 1 October 1942. These newly applied rings often gave the appearance of being lighter and wider than the original RAF type 'C1' roundel yellow ring. (Wolfe)

there on 10 June 1942. The Air Echelon arrived on 25 June and travelled by train to Atcham and High Ercall RAF stations in England. There Spitfire Mk V B fighters were handed over to the pilots (although some Mk II and Mk V As were used initially for training*).

## CAMOUFLAGE

All Spitfires received by the 31st FG were in the RAF Temperate Land Scheme, although some may have had *Mixed Grey* substituted for *Ocean Grey*. *Mixed Grey* dated from the RAF's change from green & brown upper surfaces to green & grey in August 1941. (see appendix 5)

## NATIONAL MARKINGS

One of the ground staff's first jobs was to replace the RAF roundels with USAAF white star on blue disk cocardes (see Appendix 1). USAAF cocardes were specified as being a minimum of 20" in diameter with increases in size, as required, by 5" steps. The 30" size best suited the Spitfire fuselage. The simplest method of creating the fuselage cocarde was for the RAF type 'C1' roundel to have it's yellow ring painted out and the remaining 32" shape modified to a blue and white cocarde. Just as frequently the 2" yellow ring remained. 307th FS aircraft in particular, frequently had 'correct' 30" cocardes, while with the 308th and 309th 32" was more common. The under wing RAF 32" type 'C' roundels were generally modified to 32" cocardes on the starboard side and painted out on the port side, although some examples of the more correct 30" size have been recorded. On the upper wing, a 40" size is the most common sighted in photographs. The existing upper wing

Staff Sergeant Olin M Battles gives this Spitfire Mk V of the 309th FS a 60-hour inspection at Chichester, England in 1942. (Ethell)

Engines running, Spitfires of the 307th FS line up for take-off. (Turk)

---

* Bruce Robertson

Derwood K Smith displays the damage to his Spitfire's wing received on a mission defending the Dieppe raid. Smith flew with 'B' Flight 308th FS as wing-man to Frank Hill this particular day. Note the 40" upper wing cocarde (F Hill)

307th FS crew chiefs pose beside a Spitfire Mk V wearing a 30", nominal diameter, U.S. star with yellow outer ring. (Luzzi)

roundels were painted out with *Dark Green* or *Ocean Grey* and a new cocarde applied above the port wing. It does not pay to take a one-size-fits-all approach to describing USAAF Spitfire cocardes as they were field applied in England and did vary.

On 1 October 1942 the 8th AF ordered all its aircraft be given 2" yellow borders to their national insignia and so for those Spitfires from which these had been removed, they were to be reinstated. This appears to have been done on a few 31st FG aircraft prior to the Group relinquishing it's aircraft and embarking for Operation Torch.

## SQUADRON CODES AND THEATRE MARKINGS

The other important markings to be applied were 24" high Sky squadron code letters, 'MX', 'HL' and 'WZ' for the 307th, 308th and 309th FS respectively. These followed RAF practice and were forward of the fuselage cocarde on the port side and to the rear on the starboard. Similar individual aircraft code letters were applied on the other side of the cocarde, but styles varied.

The RAF Fighter Command theatre markings of *Sky* 18" rear fuselage band and spinner plus *Ident. Yellow* wing leading edge strips were retained.

## TRAINING ON SPITFIRES

Prior to the pilots of the 31st FG training in England, they had been accustomed to the P-39's broad track and tricycle landing gear, but with the Spitfire they were faced with a narrow, conventional undercarriage and non-steerable tail wheel. Additionally, the Spitfire had weak brakes and a spade-shaped control column grip (as distinct from the American style pistol grip). It had no aileron trim tabs and some of the first training aircraft even lacked radios! Aside from their

This well known staged 'scramble' shows Harrison Thyng sitting in the cockpit of a Spitfire Mk VB as other pilots sprint for their aircraft – note the smiling faces. Running, from the left are Lieutenant Barber, unknown, 1st Lieutenant Harry L Barr, Lieutenant Mitchim, Captain John H Paulk, unknown.

*Dark Green* has been used to paint out the old RAF yellow ring around the fuselage insignia and fin flash. (IWM)

new aircraft, the pilots had to contend with the unpredictable English weather, low visibility, and the patch-work-quilt geography of England – all so different to home. Returning from a sortie to find one's base on this totally alien landscape was often filled with as much excitement as combat itself. Accidents did happen and a number of pilots were killed in this operational training period. Yet the 31st FG began to get the feel of this famous fighter and the Germans reminded them of the nearness of the air-war when air raid sirens and exploding bombs were heard on some nights.

All ranks learned to cope with English food and smoking outdoors was banned at night to prevent the chance of Luftwaffe bomber pilots seeing the tell-tale glow! While enlisted men lived in tents and walked miles to be fed or use a toilet, officers complained about the lack of central heating in buildings.

## FIRST MISSION

On 26 July 1942, less than two months after their arrival in England, members of the 31st FG flew their first practice sweep over the English Channel alongside a Canadian squadron. They suffering their first casualty the same day with Lt. Col. A. P. Clark, Executive Officer of the 31st, shot down and captured.

On 1 August the 307 FS moved to Biggin Hill, the 308th to Kenley and the 309th to Westhampnett to train with veteran RAF squadrons. Further operations were flown leading up to 19 August 1942 when the 31st FG was honoured to be chosen by the RAF as the only USAAF Fighter Group to participate in covering the Dieppe raid. This was ahead of Groups flying the much publicised Lockheed P-38 Lightning. Although the Dieppe raid itself was a failure, the 31st FG distinguished itself when Lt. Samuel F. Junkin Jr, 309th FS, shot down a Focke Wulf Fw 190;

Lieutenant Jerry D Collinsworth of the 307th FS, Biggin Hill, August 1942. Collinsworth, who achieved ace status on Spitfires, sits in the cockpit of his Mk V$_B$ wearing RAF flying gear, including goggles with flip-up sun visor. One of the most sought after accessories for USAAF fighter pilots throughout the war was the RAF-issue oxygen mask and helmet with its silk lining, far preferred to the USAAF canvas item. This photo illustrates a case where the slightly larger RAF roundel has been painted out and a 30" nominal diameter USAAF cocarde substituted. The 2" yellow outer ring gives an overall diameter of 34". Note the light coloured exhaust staining caused by an engine tuned to run lean. (Turk)

thereby achieving the first 'kill' by a USAAF pilot in the European Theatre of Operations (ETO). Although Lt. John White also scored a victory, the overall result for the four 31st FG missions flown that day was two German aircraft destroyed for the loss of four pilots missing and one killed.

At this juncture in 1942 criticism of American designed fighters by some senior American officers and Senators back in the United States came to a head – they demanded better fighter designs. Some newspapers and magazines published articles asking why there weren't better fighters than the P-39 and P-40 which were outclassed and being rejected elsewhere. At the same time there was much favourable publicity given to USAAF fighter actions over Dieppe flying Spitfires. Some US officials became annoyed at this publicity and a political backlash developed regarding the use of foreign equipment by the Army Air Forces.

## RUMOURS

In September 1942 the men of the 31st FG noticed a sudden change of status as they passed from RAF to USAAF control. Combat missions were flown, but in addition to full uniform inspections and a combination of boring marches and tedious drills, rumours circulated that 'Top Brass' had something in mind for the Group – and they did. In early October the Group was transferred to the Twelfth Fighter Command (XII FC) of the newly created Twelfth Air Force (12th AF) and, later in the month, the men were divided into small groups, with some being posted to undisclosed destinations. One of these groups was an advance party sent to Gibraltar where new Spitfire Mk V (trop) fighters awaited them for Operation Torch – the Anglo/American invasion of North Africa.

Two views of what appears to be the same Spitfire Mk V$_B$.

**Above**, when flown by Captain Frank Hill of the 308 FS in the summer of 1942 while the squadron was based at Kenley. **Below**, 'HL-C' when flown by Lt, Edward Dalrymple at Tangmere, July 1942. Note the blunt style de Havilland spinner, compared with the more common, longer, Rotol one fitted to most Mk Vs. (F Hill, above; E Dalrymple, below)

# OPERATION TORCH – NORTH AFRICA

## GIBRALTAR

On 21 October 1942 the pilots were sent north from their English bases by train to Greenock, Scotland, where they boarded HMS Leinster. They were joined on board by the 52nd FG and nine RAF fighter squadrons, then HMS Leinster joined a convoy of ships and sailed for Gibraltar, the British territory on the southern tip of Spain. Awaiting the 31st on Gibraltar's airfields, were Spitfire Mk V (trop) fighters with their bulky Volkes tropical dust filters. The filter, while improving engine life, ruined the slim lines of the Spitfire and was not liked by the pilots because it reduced the Spitfire Mk V's maximum speed by approximately 14 mph.

Del Avery of the 31st FG and Gene Keyes of the 52nd FG sitting on a Spitfire Mk VB still in its RAF markings, Gibraltar, November 1942. RAF, FAA and USAAF units all repainted their aircraft in Operation Torch markings in Gibraltar. (Deaton)

## DESERT CAMOUFLAGE

The new Spitfires were received in British national markings and RAF Desert Scheme camouflage of *Dark Earth* and *Mid-Stone* upper surfaces with *Azure Blue* lower surfaces. As in England, back in July, the ground staff's first job was to alter the RAF roundels to USAAF cocardes, apply unit codes and paint over the RAF fin flashes. The 9th AF, which also operated in North Africa, painted RAF-style fin flashes on its aircraft, but not so the new 12th AF*. Upper wing roundels were replaced with cocardes, usually of 45" nominal diameter, plus an additional yellow ring. This yellow ring varied in width with 2-3 inches being common. Fuselage cocardes were modified from the existing 36" RAF type 'C1' roundels and the under-wing RAF type 'C' roundels were generally given a yellow ring and modified to cocardes. As an additional recognition marking for the benefit of the Moroccan population, a temporary American flag decal was applied to both sides of the fuselage around the cockpit area, the exact location varying. Spinners and 24" code letters on 31st FG aircraft in the Mediterranean Theatre of Operation

North Africa

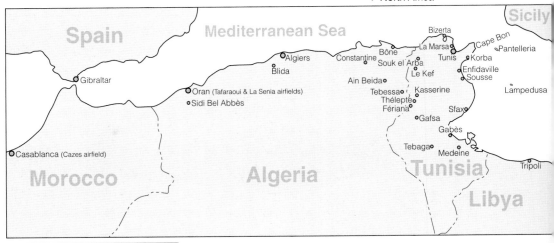

---

\* Dana Bell

This frequently published photo shows Spitfires of the 31st or 52nd FG in Gibraltar. These particular aircraft still have their fin flashes which were rarely recorded on 12th AF aircraft. The 9th AF did apply RAF-style fin flashes to its aircraft. (via B Anderson)

(MTO) were specified as white at this time. Remember, all these markings were field-applied in a hurry.

## OPERATION TORCH

The 31st FG was now briefed for its part in Operation Torch by the staff of Major General James Doolittle, commander of the newly-created 12th Air Force. As a step to wresting Europe back from the Germans, the Allies chose to invade French North Africa, west of where the British 8th Army was pushing the German Afrika Korps and Italian armies westward into Libya and, ultimately, Tunisia.

The Operation Torch landings commenced on 8 November 1942 and, although it was an Allied action, it was foremost America's first vast concentration of ground forces to be committed against Axis forces. However, there was the complicating background of the diplomatic

Lieutenant Louis N Macomber enjoys a cigarette in front of his Spitfire Mk V somewhere in North Africa. The crude markings and yellow surround to the fuselage star date the photo as shortly after the Torch landings. Note the small white 'X' which was on a number of Operation Torch Spitfires. It occurs too frequently to be an individual aircraft code letter. (Turk)

interests of Vichy France, America and Great Britain. The Nazis did not occupy southern France after defeating the French in 1940. Rather, they allowed them to form a government in the southern French city of Vichy and from there govern their colonial territories, such as those in North Africa. In exchange the Nazis extracted the concession that the Vichy Government would oppose British interests. The United States maintained discreet diplomatic relations with the Vichy Government and understood the Vichy Government might not oppose American interests as strongly as those of Great Britain. This was one reason why British aircraft participating in Torch were painted with pseudo American markings. (see colour illustration, page 36)

The landings took place at Casablanca in Morocco, and at Oran and Algiers in Algeria; countries governed from Vichy France and garrisoned by capable military units. Yet there was no guarantee – right up till the moment that Operation Torch began – that French forces would not fight the Americans.

The 31st FG's job was to protect the invasion forces at Oran, Algeria and, if fuel was low, to land at Tafaraoui or La Senia airfields near Oran. Sea Hurricanes, flying from British carriers in the invasion fleet, were to gain initial air superiority and there was the presumption that Vichy French air bases near Oran would be under the control of the Sea Hurricanes, by the time the 31st FG Spitfires arrived over their designated airfields.

On 8 November 1942, the 31st FG flew from Gibraltar expecting to land unopposed at Tafaraoui, Algeria, but they were attacked by Vichy French Dewoitine D 520's. This particular D 520 was used as a hack by the 31st FG pilots while based at Tafaraoui or La Senia. Note the unusual angle of the USAAF star and retention of the French rudder markings. (Mandli)

General Doolittle taxis a 308th FS Spitfire Mk Vʙ (trop) from this damaged former French hangar at Tafaraoui, Algeria, November 1942. (Turk)

## THE TORCH LANDINGS

On 8 November 1942 the Operation Torch landings began. But instead of Sea Hurricanes protecting their airfield, four Vichy French Dewoitine 520 fighters resisted the American Spitfires, shooting one down, killing the pilot. Major Harrison Thyng and Lt. Carl Payne shot down two of the Dewoitines and then landed at Tafaraoui, which had been captured by American paratroopers. The following day the French shelled Tafaraoui airfield for 18 minutes and made the Allies all too well aware of the Vichy force's fascist loyalties.

More Vichy French resistance appeared at Casablanca and Algiers. But there were difficulties in keeping the Spitfires flying because the Group's ground echelon had been landed in Algeria by ship and was then forced to make a lengthy march inland to Tafaraoui. There were problems associated with gathering the entire Group together, housing and feeding them and generating a new battle plan consistent with the changing war situation. To supply the aircraft at Tafaraoui with war matériel some men purloined usable French ammunition and fuel for the Spitfires. On 9 November a French Foreign Legion (FFL) armoured column was reported heading north toward Oran from its base at Sidi Bel Abbès. Pilots of the 31st FG therefore flew several missions against the FFL and by destroying much mechanized equipment, prevented any further advance.

The remaining French forces around Casablanca and Oran ceased fighting a few days later. But it was not until 13 November that negotiations with the highest French officials in North Africa brought about an agreement that Vichy forces in Morocco and Algeria would switch to the Allied side. The Allies negotiations with the Vichy French regarding Tunisia were finalised by 18 November. However, in France the Vichy government remained loyal to the Nazis. During this time

Members of the 31st FG outside the French Foreign Legion Headquarters in Sidi Bel Abbès, south of Oran, November 1942. (F Hill)

there were a few raids by the Luftwaffe, but essentially all resistance to the American forces in western North Africa came from Vichy French forces. Once that crisis had passed, General Dwight D Eisenhower's Allied armies prepared to march east to trap the still large Axis forces between themselves and General Montgomery's 8th Army.

The 31st FG was transferred to the bomb-pitted airfield at La Senia, near Oran on 14 November. After making this modern but battle-damaged airfield serviceable, much of the remainder of the month was spent helping consolidate the Allies' position, with the 31st FG flying air defence sorties and convoy protection patrols. Conditions were primitive, to say the least, surrounded by desert with the rainy season about to begin which would soon turn unpaved desert roads into muddy quagmires. The officers lived in former French barracks while the enlisted men lived in tents.

In early December 1942 Colonel Fred M Dean relieved Colonel John Hawkins as 31st FG Commander.

One squadron of the 52nd FG had been posted directly into combat far to the east, leaving pilots of the 31st wondering why they had not been given first crack at the Axis air forces, rather than their less experienced comrades. On 17 November the 31st made a short stop at Algiers and then flew on to Bône in Algeria. On 21 December the 307th and 308th FS flew east to Maison Blanche airfield near Algiers while the 309th remained at La Senia.

Lt. Montooth, Armament Officer of the 307th FS, La Senia, 1943. Note the Desert camouflaged Spitfire behind him with the code letter 'W' looking more like an up-side-down 'M' (Turk)

Although designed as a point defence interceptor, there was an obvious need to improve the Spitfire's range in North Africa to provide more tactical flexibility, essentially time over target or patrol time. Jettisonable slipper tanks, mounted under the belly were available in various sizes: 30, 45 and 90 gallon, to improve tactical flexibility. The 31st FG frequently used the 90 gallon tanks on their Spitfire Mk V (trop) aircraft which improved their maximum range from 425 miles to 1060 miles. Throughout the war the British aircraft industry manufactured over 300,000 drop-tanks, but supplies were not always on hand at the front line. Some missions from Algiers, and later, were flown with the scarce tanks installed. However they did knock 17 mph off the maximum speed, and needed to be jettisoned before combat.

## PLANNING FOR VICTORY

In January 1943 one of the most significant Allied conferences of the war was held at Casablanca in Morocco with Roosevelt, Churchill and generals and admirals participating representing all Western Allies. Without being told why, the 308th FS was ordered to Cazes airfield, near Casablanca. Eventually the pilots learned that they were to have the honour of being airborne escorts to the leaders attending this crucial conference and fly protective patrols overhead throughout.

Late in January 1943 the 309th FS moved to Orleansville, Algeria, and in February the 308th returned from Cazes to La Senia but, at the same time, prepared to move east to the large air base at Thelepte, Tunisia. The 307th FS was at Orleansville and Maison Blanche. The three squadrons were to meet at Thelepte on 8 February 1943, relieving the 33rd FG P-40's (which were now considered obsolete as frontline fighters). This latest move brought the 31st FG close to the rear of the strong Allied forces pursuing the Afrika Corps in Tunisia. As there had been little recent combat and the war in North Africa was reaching a successful conclusion, some members of the group believed that the war in Europe would end in 1943. However, the most fierce fighting still lay ahead for the pilots of the 31st FG .The front lines were only a

Lieutenant Colonel Fred Dean, stands with his Spitfire Mk VB (trop) at La Senia, Algeria. This aircraft was coded 'F-MD' and had a white spinner with black backing plate. Dean succeeded Colonel John Hawkins as commanding officer of the 31st FG on 5 December 1942. (Hagins)

Lamar W Davis Jr. of the 309th FS in his Spitfire Mk V, 18 January 1943. Note the emergency crowbar clipped inside the door. (L W Davis)

Proof that a sharks-mouth makes any aircraft look aggressive (or comical). The bulky tropical filter allowed space for this 307th FS Spitfire Mk Vc (trop) at La Senia to have this red and white sharks mouth applied. Note the eye painted on the 20mm cannon, taped over gun ports and the circular intake to the oil cooler under the port wing. This is often incorrectly depicted as a half-round on model kits. That shape is only correct for Spitfire Mk I/II variants. (Turk)

few dozen miles east of Thelepte. Also, the Luftwaffe were not solely on the defensive and being so near to the frontlines artillery fire could be heard from both the Allied and German sides! Thelepte was extremely crowded with P-40's Spitfires, the French Lafayette Escadrille (flying P-40's supplied by the U.S.) and squadrons of the 52nd FG. In the air, the 31st flew escort for A-20 Boston's and reconnaissance P-39 Airacobras.

The Tunisian campaign suddenly became critical along the American front on 15 February as German forces began a determined counter-attack at Kasserine Pass. A big air battle that day saw the 31st FG claim five enemy aircraft for the loss of one. Messerschmitt Bf 109's and Focke Wulf Fw 190's strafed Thelepte. At approximately 2.30AM on 17 February the 31st FG was told to quit the airfield as soon as possible because German troops were literally coming up the road. Spitfires that were serviceable were flown off in total darkness to the airfield at Tebessa, about 50 miles

Another Sharks-mouth Spitfire Mk Vc (trop) of the 307th FS at La Senia in North Africa, November 1942. Note the tires decorated with white walls. The aircraft appears to be having its engine run up. (Turk)

west, in Algeria. Those not serviceable were burned. The men left behind were told to gather up as much useful matériel as possible, load the squadrons few trucks and move in darkness to Youks-les-Bains and Tebessa. In the stress, confusion and haste conflicting orders were issued and some squadron records and lots of equipment were left behind in the rush to evade capture. German artillery shells hit the field near dawn while men were still loading equipment and to this day the veterans involved still talk about this rapid evacuation in hushed tones.

On 21 February, with the German threat continuing, the planes and men had to be evacuated even further to the northwest, moving from Tebessa to Du Kouif. Major John White of the 307th FS destroyed two enemy aircraft that day. This same day the Germans pounded

One of America's greatest fighter pilots, Major Harrison Thyng, while Commanding Officer of the 309th FS between 30 January and 12 May 1943. Thyng achieved Ace status in WWII and again while flying F-86 Sabres in Korea. This Desert Scheme Spitfire Mk V has 32" fuselage cocardes and white code letters. (Thyng)

Spitfire Mk Vs of the 309th FS taxi line abreast in the desert dust at Thelepte, Tunisia. (Hagins)

**Right** and **below**. Captain Frank Hill while he was a flight commander with the 308th FS, Thelepte, Tunisia, February 1943. Despite being a desert airstrip the winter weather was not warm. Hill is wearing a sheep skin lined jacket and his crew chief below also has winter clothing on. This Spitfire Mk Vв (trop), still in it's original desert camouflage, is highly polished which tended to give the aircraft a darker appearance. Note the factory applied serial number has not been overpainted, as happened with field repainted USAAF Spitfires. The individual aircraft code letter is repeated under the nose. (F Hill)

Another Spitfire MkV, serial ES306, flown by Captain Frank Hill, Thelepte, Tunisia, February/March 1943. Note the primitive, unprepared air strip, with a crew bunker visible in the right background. (F Hill)

Major Frank Hill flew this Spitfire Mk VB (trop) ER187 when he commanded the 309th FS between 12 May and 12 July 1943 in North Africa. It is connected to a starter trolley while on alert. The photo was taken the same time as that at the top of page 26. (F Hill)

Captain Frank Hill, when he was with the 309th FS. He has had just had the swastika denoting his fifth kill painted on this Spitfire Mk V<sub>B</sub> (trop) on 6 May 1943 at La Senia. Note his personal marking 'Lindy and Frank' above the row of kill markings and this aircraft's custom-fitted internal rear-view mirror. (F Hill)

Colonel Fred Dean, Commander of the 31st FG, briefs pilots for a mission at Thelepte airfield, Tunisia, spring 1943. This kind of camouflaged dugout was the norm on desert airstrips in North Africa. (via P Ludwig)

American ground forces at the disastrous battle of Kasserine Pass, but the 31st FG was only able to fly one supporting mission due to very poor weather. The 31st FG became scattered in this period, with headquarters conducting another move to Canrobert, Algeria, while some of the planes and pilots were at Youks, and a few members of the group were still back at La Senia. While the rapid advance of the Allied armies in Tunisia stalled, general chaos and lost equipment cut into the high morale of the men.

## FINALE IN TUNISIA

More missions were flown to Kasserine in attempts to halt the Axis and the 31st FG was ordered to assemble at Kalaa Djerda in Tunisia on 24 February 1943 to help push back the German's concerted counter attack. Constant missions were flown against German forces with ground attack and bomb-line patrols and Kasserine was back in U.S. hands by 25 February. Success by the Allied armies began to take its toll on the Africa Korps and on 8 March 1943 the 31st FG was able to return to Thelepte, with escorts of P-39s and A-20s on armed reconnaissance being their main job.

The crisis caused by the German counter-attack began to wane and the final great battle for control of North Africa moved ahead – there would be no setbacks for the Allies this time. During mid March

**Below**. Major Frank Hill poses with his Spitfire at Korba North, Cape Bon, Tunisia, late June 1943. The aircraft exhibits Hill's final combat score with $6\frac{1}{2}$ confirmed, plus 3 shared with his wingman and 4 probables. The names in white above his kill markings are 'Lindy and Frank'. Note that the aircraft's fuselage star-and-bar has a red outline by this date. (F Hill)

1943 the 31st FG began one of its busiest periods since arriving in North Africa, flying as many as six missions each day, frequently escorting medium bombers. Everyone sensed that the end was near for the German and Italian forces being bottled up at Gabès in Tunisia. However, the fighting was fierce till the bitter end of this drawn out campaign.

After several more moves to small airfields in Tunisia during March and a glimpse of new Spitfire Mk IX's operated by an RAF squadron; the 31st FG moved to Sbeitla on 7 April. By the middle of the month a dozen of these more capable Spitfires had been received by the Group.

Major Frank Hill downed two enemy aircraft on 22 April, by which time the 31st FG had lost three pilots killed, three missing, four as Prisoners of War and one seriously wounded in the North African campaign. Yet the Group had destroyed more enemy aircraft than it lost, with 11 claimed on 6 May alone. All the top guns, including: Lt. Colonel Harrison Thyng 309th FS, Captain Jerry Collinsworth 307th FS, Capt. Carl Payne 309th FS and Lt. Charles Fischette 307th FS contributed and the Group received congratulatory messages from High Command.

On 10 May the Tunisian campaign finally ended. The 31st FG moved twice more before settling at Korba, near Cape Bon on 20 May, its ninth base in just four months. At last many of the Groups Spitfire Mk Vs were exchanged for the more capable Mk IXs. Later, in August 1943, some Mk VIIIs were also received and the 308th FS eventually entirely re-equipped with them. However, the Spitfire Mk Vs soldiered on and were still listed on 31st FG mission reports well into 1944.

Also present at Korba was an RAF Air-Sea-Rescue squadron flying another Reginald Mitchell designed aircraft, the Supermarine Walrus flying boat, used to pluck downed pilots from the Mediterranean.

On 31 May 1943 Lieutenant Colonel Dean issued copies of a memorandum he had prepared for Lieutenant General Carl Spaatz which summarised the Groups recent activity. Dean stated that to that date the 31st FG 'have destroyed 55 enemy aircraft, probably destroyed 18

Supermarine Walrus flying boats in the air. See text this page. (J O'Sullivan)

Spitfire Mk IXc 'MX-D' of the 307th FS at an unknown North African airstrip in 1943. EN307 is an early production Mk IX with the small style carburettor intake. This machine was eventually lost over Italy on 15 December 1943*. Note the roughly made shroud over the exhausts which may have been to exclude sand from the engine, when not running, on the ground. (Luzzi)

* Morgan and Shacklady.

and damaged 61, for the loss of 19 pilots, 10 of whom are known to be Prisoners of War. I think we have an unsurpassed record.' Nine aircraft were shot down by the enemy but, as was so often the case when operating under arduous conditions, 14 more had been lost in accidents. The ferocity of the North African campaign was noted in Dean's dry statistics. Seven enemy aircraft were shot down between 8 November 1942 and 18 February 1943 and 46 were claimed during the most active period, between 18 February and 15 May 1943. This contrasted with just two during the Group's months in England. Lieutenant Colonel Dean was awarded the Silver Star for his outstanding leadership and, by this stage, Major Frank Hill and Lieutenant Colonel Harrison R Thyng (Group Executive Officer) had both achieved Ace status.

## OPERATION FLAX

The story of the air war in Tunisia would be incomplete without mention of Operation Flax – the concerted Allied opposition of Axis attempts to re-supply and evacuate the Afrika Korps from Tunisia in the final battle for North Africa. Flax began on 5 April with the 82nd FG, equipped with P-38 Lightnings, escorting B-25 Mitchells flying a sea sweep in the morning northeast of the Cape Bon Peninsula. Pilots spotted a fleet of 31 Ju 52 three-engine German transports, lumbering slowly south to Tunis, escorted by nearly as many fighters. Seven Ju 52's and eight escorts were shot down. P-38's of the 1st FG entered the fray and shot down 11 more transports and fighters.

German re-supply flights using unarmed, vulnerable transports into an area where Allied air superiority was now complete and Intelligence timely, proved a tragedy for the helpless German air crews.

A Spitfire MK IX being given its 100 hour inspection during the hottest part of the summer in North Africa. Note the five victory markings under the wind screen and the white cloth doped over the cannon and machine gun ports to keep out the dust. (Hagins)

On 10 April the Luftwaffe tried again. The 1st FG was up at dawn that day and intercepted a huge air armada of 59 Italian transports escorted by fifteen Italian and German fighters. Ten transports and two escorts were shot down. Later in the day the carnage continued when P-38's found Ju 52s and some of the massive, six-engine, Me 323 transports and shot down eleven in total. Allied planners predicted the desperate measures taken by the Germans and Italians to shore up their precarious situation in North Africa and planned accordingly. The Allies successful blockade, which included submarine and air patrols, northeast of Cape Bon, effectively denied the Axis armies re-supply. The Germans again attempted supply and evacuation missions on 11, 18, and 19 April. On the 18th, P-40's of the 57th FG and 324th FG, accompanied by Spitfires of 92 Squadron RAF, were up patrolling near dusk when the largest fleet of transports yet was intercepted. Sixty-five Ju 52s and a mixed Italian and German fighter escort were caught leaving Tunisia for Sicily and a slaughter began. The transports tried to retire before being shot down, but to no avail. Counting those shot down and others which crash-landed, 59 transports were destroyed. Many of the escorts were also shot down and the day became known as 'The Palm Sunday Massacre'

Two South African Air Force squadrons, No's 2 and 5 flying P-40 Kittyhawks, were up on the 19th to continue the disaster for the enemy; so that when Operation Flax was complete over 400 transport aircraft had been shot down, dooming the Afrika Korps.

For the 31st FG the question remained as to why their American Spitfire Mk IXs had never been assigned to participate in Operation Flax at any time; while this fish-in-a-barrel shooting was being enjoyed by USAAF units flying American-built fighters, sometimes with RAF Spitfires providing top cover.

Major George LaBreche, Commanding Officer of the 307th FS, photographed no earlier than mid April 1943, in the cockpit of his Spitfire. Note the Squadron's insignia beneath the cockpit. (Turk)

## PANTELLERIA

A potential thorn in the side for Allied forces invading Sicily, north across the Mediterranean, was the small Italian held island of Pantelleria – just 40 miles northeast of Cape Bon. Pantelleria airfield featured an underground hangar (capable of protecting 50 aircraft) which had proven immune to high-level precision bombing. Italian and German aircraft regularly emerged from this deep, cave-like, hangar to harass the Allies. The Allies had thrown considerable force against the island, trying to bomb its garrison into submission, with a campaign commencing on 14 May 1943. The 31st FG joined that assault, escorting bombers on 6 June from their Korba airfield. That day the Group claimed 11 enemy aircraft downed, Major Hill getting two. The following day, enemy fighter-bombers replied, strafing the 31st FG base at Korba causing considerable damage and wounding many enlisted men.

In his book on the 31st FG, Major Rolland G Lamensdorf describes how High Command ordered the 31st FG to fly one Spitfire over Pantelleria at low altitude to look for signs of surrender – there were none and so the intense aerial assault against Pantelleria continued. On 10 June the 307th FS destroyed seven enemy aircraft. Because of this good hunting, the 309th FS provided 12 Spitfire Mk Vs and 6 Mk IXs on 11 June as high cover for B-17, B-25, A-20 and P-39 bombers while P-40's acted as close escort. Thirteen Macchi MC.202's, some Bf 109's and three Fw 190's attacked and in the ensuing dog-fight the 309th destroyed seven Axis aircraft. The sustained weight of missions eventually achieved air superiority over Pantelleria and the island surrendered without an invasion being necessary.

Major Lamensdorf noted that the 31st FG had destroyed 27 enemy aircraft and lost just four in this short, but intense, campaign. Major John White claimed three, while Captain Royal N Baker (later a jet ace in Korea), Captain Jerry Collinsworth and Major Fischette each claimed two.

A 308th FS Spitfire Mk Vc, somewhere in North Africa. This aircraft has been repainted in a nonstandard colour scheme, possibly dark green and brown upper surfaces with light blue undersurfaces. This was seen as a field repaint scheme on some Allied Spitfires from the Sicilian campaign onwards. 'HL-B' is fitted with the stubby de Havilland spinner and propeller. (Hagins)

# SICILY

## INVASION

In June 1943 the continuing expansion of the USAAF saw the 31st FG reassigned to the 64th Fighter Wing (which was commanded by the Group's former leader, Colonel Hawkins).

To be as near as possible to support the next stage of the Allied advance, the invasion of Sicily, the 31st FG moved to the island of Gozo, adjacent to Malta which, with great sacrifice, had remained in British hands. The 31st FG's new air field had been carved out of vineyards on Gozo and was just 60 miles from Sicily. The Group flew in on 30 June and were serviced, temporarily, by RAF ground crews. Timing for the Sicily invasion required the Groups ground echelon to be transported to Guyetville and Tunis seaports and from there they were to be landed in Sicily, once the army had stabilized the ground situation.

Action for the 31st FG commenced over Sicily on 6 July as USAAF bombers escorted by the Group's Spitfires softened up German positions. On the 9th the pilots witnessed the largest Allied convoy they had ever seen, forming for the invasion scheduled for 10 July. The Group successfully intercepted Axis air raids against the convoy on 10 and 11 July, however the Spitfire pilots experienced intense flak coming from their own ships! Overall, relativity few enemy aircraft were seen during the initial Sicilian landings.

When the 31st FG were allocated a captured airfield at Ponte Olivo, North of Gela, Sicily, they became the first American fighter group to land on Sicilian soil.

In mid-July Frank Hill was promoted to command the Group, while Colonel Fred Dean, after nearly eight months on operations, returned to the United States where he joined the advisory staff of General Arnold in Washington D.C.

Wing Commander Brian Kingcombe, on the left, of the RAF's Desert Air Force, with Major Frank Hill. Kingcombe had achieved ace status in the Battle of Britain and led the 308th FS on its initial combat missions over Europe in 1942. This photograph was taken at Termini, Sicily, in August 1943 and shows Kingcombe's Spitfire Mk VIII, coded with his initials 'BK', as was the custom for RAF Officers of Wing Commander rank and higher. Note the aircraft's faded desert camouflage scheme of *Dark Earth* and *Mid Stone* upper surfaces, with *Azure Blue* lower surfaces. A Wing Commanders pennant is painted beneath the wind screen. (F Hill)

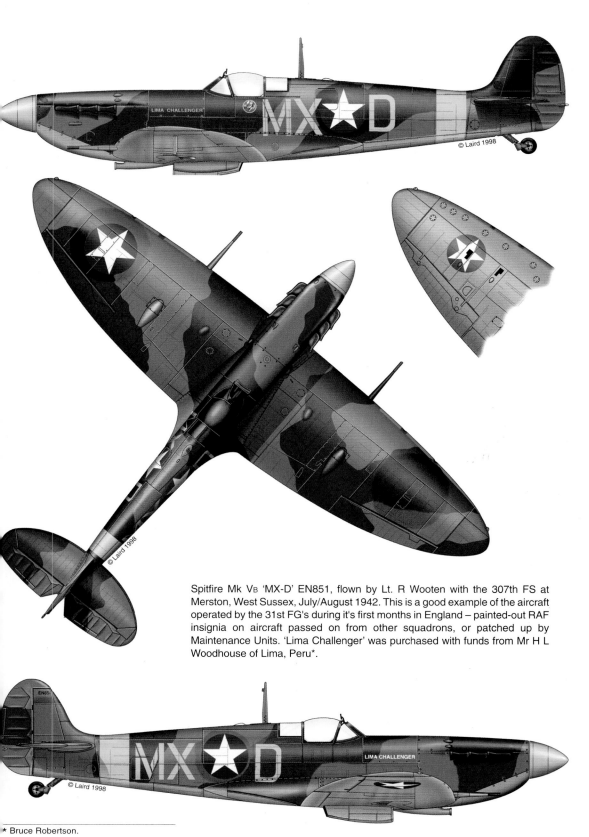

Spitfire Mk V<sub>B</sub> 'MX-D' EN851, flown by Lt. R Wooten with the 307th FS at Merston, West Sussex, July/August 1942. This is a good example of the aircraft operated by the 31st FG's during it's first months in England – painted-out RAF insignia on aircraft passed on from other squadrons, or patched up by Maintenance Units. 'Lima Challenger' was purchased with funds from Mr H L Woodhouse of Lima, Peru*.

<hr>

* Bruce Robertson.

## New National Markings

During this period the 31st FG operated a mixture of Spitfire Mk V, VIII, and IX fighters camouflaged in the RAF Desert scheme. From 28 June 1943, USAAF aircraft were required to add white rectangles either side of the existing cocardes with an *Insignia Red* border. For Spitfires operated in the MTO this meant over-painting the existing yellow rings, adding the white rectangles and then a 2" red border. In theory the end result of the change would be Spitfires with cocardes 34" high overall (30" nominal diameter) in all four positions. Needless to say, this didn't happen overnight and examples abound of Spitfires with rectangles but no borders.

A further change, ordered on 14 August while the 31st FG was still based on Sicily, was the replacement of red with *Insignia Blue* as the border colour. This change was for the benefit of American aircraft operating in the Pacific where 'red' equated with 'Japanese'. Also, late in 1943 all Allied fighters in the MTO had their white spinners repainted red – this applying to RAF operated aircraft as well.

## Camouflage

On Sicily, examples of aircraft repainted at unit level with green and brown or green and grey upper surfaces began to appear; particularly the older Spitfire Mk Vs, although *new* replacement aircraft were still delivered in RAF Desert camouflage.

Colonel Fred M Dean on the day he relinquished command of the 31st FG to Lt. Colonel Frank Hill, July 1943, Ponte Olivo, Sicily. Colonel Dean is standing on the wing of his Spitfire Mk Vc (trop) coded F-MD on the port side and FM-D on the starboard. Lt. Colonel Hill is standing at the wing root. Both are well tanned by the Mediterranean sun. Note the hole behind the exhaust stacks where, in cooler climates a tube would take hot exhaust air and route it to heat the guns. (F Hill)

A 309th FS Spitfire Mk IX fitted with a 90-gallon slipper tank at Termini, Sicily, August 1943. The machine appears to be an early production Mk IXc with its carburettor intake removed at the time the photograph was taken.

The pilots crouching in front of the aircraft are, from the left; Lieutenant Donald Keith, Hank Hughes, Harry Trifon (flight surgeon), Dale Shaffer Jr. and Carl Payne. (Payne was C.O. of the 309th FS from 13 July to 14 October 1943. (J Fawcett)

Captain Harry L Barr of the 309th FS, is congratulated by his crew chief S/Sergeant Jay W Sisco after his 'kill' of 12 July 1943. Barr had achieved this success over the 5th Army battle front. Eight days earlier, the 31st FG had destroyed six and damaged two enemy aircraft in a single days combat. (USAAF)

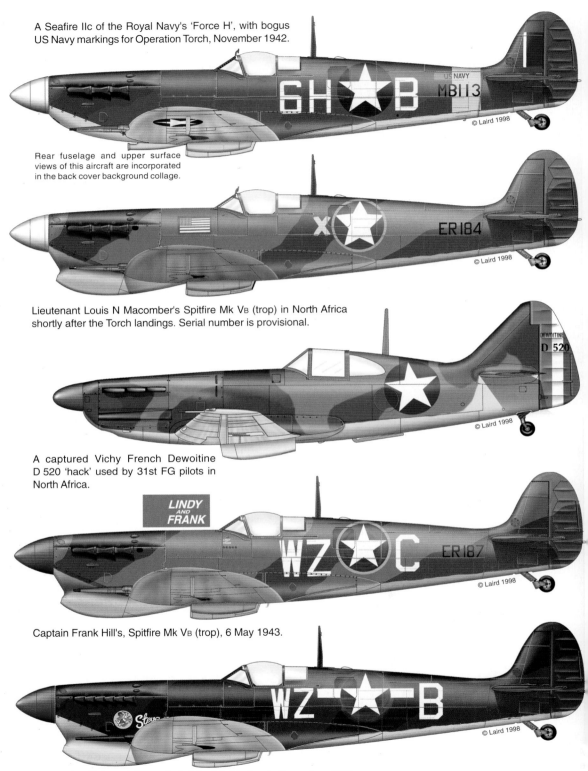

A Seafire IIc of the Royal Navy's 'Force H', with bogus US Navy markings for Operation Torch, November 1942.

Rear fuselage and upper surface views of this aircraft are incorporated in the back cover background collage.

Lieutenant Louis N Macomber's Spitfire Mk VB (trop) in North Africa shortly after the Torch landings. Serial number is provisional.

A captured Vichy French Dewoitine D 520 'hack' used by 31st FG pilots in North Africa.

Captain Frank Hill's, Spitfire Mk VB (trop), 6 May 1943.

Lieutenant Robert J Connor's Spitfire Mk Vc (trop), December 1943. Code letter 'B' is provisional

2nd Lieutenant William Skinner with his Crew Chief stand in front of their Spitfire Mk Vc July/August 1943. Note the nonstandard application of the red border around the 30" nominal diameter fuselage cocarde and customised, internal, rear-view mirror. (W Skinner)

An early production Spitfire Mk IXc with the small carburettor intake, 1943. This 307th FS machine exhibits many signs of field part-modified RAF roundels repainted to represent USAAF cocardes, with red centres painted out, yellow border applied to the lower wing marking and white paint used to achieve a star. (W Skinner)

Two Spitfire Mk Vs of the 308th FS over the Mediterranean. Note the repetition of the code letter 'A' which later became a common practice in the 31st FG. (IWM)

Lt. Colonel Frank Hill with his desert camouflaged Spitfire Mk IXc, Millazzo airfield, Sicily, September 1943. Hill followed the RAF custom and changed his code letters to his initials 'FA-H', in 20" high white letters, when he was promoted to command the 31st FG.

Even at this stage of the war many American aircraft still carried a mustard coloured patch of gas-sensitive paint, seen here above the rear bar of the fuselage star-and-bar. The patch changed colour when exposed to poison gas. (F Hill)

## VICTORY IN SICILY

On the political front, Italian dictator Benito Mussolini's Government had resigned on 26 July 1943. This same day the 31st FG received a Citation of Excellence from Lieutenant General Carl 'Tooey' Spaatz.

By 2 August the 31st FG was operating from Termini airfield. Six days later a mixture of their Spitfire Mk Vcs and Mk VIIIs tangled with 16-20 Fw 190 fighter-bombers and their Bf 109 escorts. Three Fw 190's were claimed for no losses.

The Sicily campaign ended on 17 August 1943 and saw Colonel Charles M McCorkle, a West Point graduate, assume command. He had earlier commanded the first (U.S. based) P-51B Mustang Group. The US based Group flew P-51Bs without extra internal fuel tanks fitted to P-51Bs serving overseas. (see photo page 56)

Italy was finally prepared to sign an armistice and on 31 August the 308th FS sent four Spitfires to escort an aircraft bringing the Italian surrender delegation to Termini airfield. The Armistice came into effect on 3 September.

On 1 September Lt. General Spaatz personally decorated several pilots with the DFC. Then the Group transferred to Milazzo airfield in eastern Sicily – much nearer the Italian mainland.

Italy and Sicily.

The 31st FG operated several high-altitude Spitfire HF Mk VIII interceptors with extended wing tips. Here 'HL-H' of the 308th FS sits on an airfield in Sicily, about August 1943. It is painted in the RAF Desert Scheme. (Wolfe)

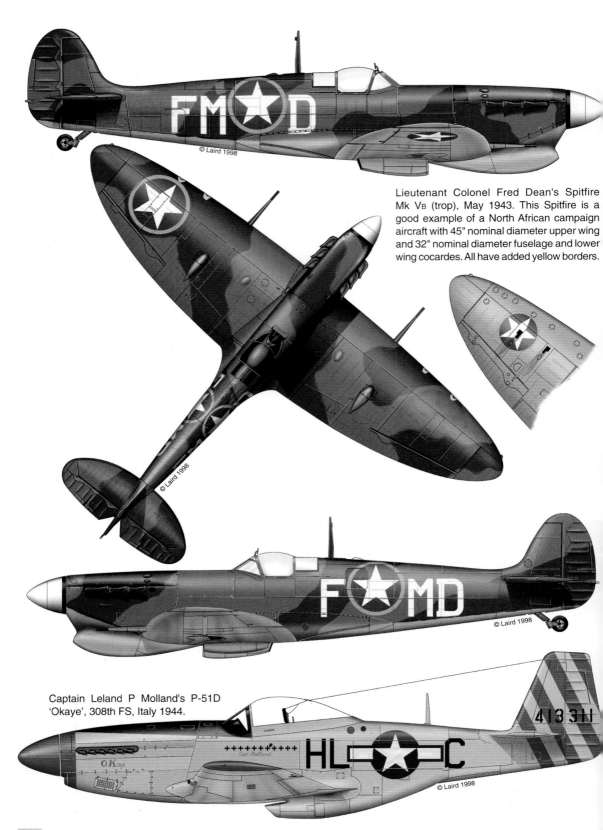

© Laird 1998

Lieutenant Colonel Fred Dean's Spitfire Mk V$_B$ (trop), May 1943. This Spitfire is a good example of a North African campaign aircraft with 45" nominal diameter upper wing and 32" nominal diameter fuselage and lower wing cocardes. All have added yellow borders.

© Laird 1998

© Laird 1998

Captain Leland P Molland's P-51D 'Okaye', 308th FS, Italy 1944.

© Laird 1998

Captain Leland P Molland's Spitfire Mk VIII at Castel Volturno, Italy, February/March 1944. Some publications have incorrectly illustrated 'Fargo Express' coded as 'HL-X'.

© Laird 1998

# ITALY

The 31st FG commenced operations over Italy on 9 September 1943, when the Allied invasion at Salerno started, along with intense daily air operations. On 10 September, the 309th FS was vectored onto 20 Bf 109s and 16 Fw 190 fighter-bombers threatening the fleet and when the Spitfires attacked, the enemy pilots dumped their bombs harmlessly. Two enemy aircraft were claimed shot down for no loss.

USAAF units were suddenly required to keep daily mission reports, including information on numbers of precious drop tanks used. There may have been more paperwork for clerks in the 31st FG in late 1943, but today's historians are glad to have the treasure of such depth of record-keeping.

The 31st FG was now regarded as one of the best fighter groups in the MTO and a decision was made to base a small portion of the Group on Italian soil as soon as enemy forces were pushed back enough to establish a landing strip. A mere two days after the invasion, ground personnel of the Group were transported by LST and landed to reconnoitre Montecorvino airfield. The men came under enemy artillery fire because of their position near British artillery. To avoid becoming a German target they were encamped at the midpoint of the trajectory of Allied and German shellfire, which passed over their heads day and night.

The wrap-around RAF Desert Scheme on this Canadian Spitfire Mk VIII, photographed on 22 January 1944, is identical to those of the 308th FS aircraft in William Skinners colour photographs on page 44. This is an early production Mk VIII with the original rounded rudder. (C Doodson)

1st Lieutenant Charles E 'Chuck' Brown, stands by the nose of his desert camouflaged Spitfire Mk VIII. Note the 90-gallon drop-tank and 308th FS insignia. (C Brown)

Not until the 18th did British and American forces drive the enemy far enough inland to make use of Montecorvino possible. On that same day a Colonel from the Third Air Support Command (III ASC), who landed at Montecorvino to evaluate it, was killed when a German artillery shell destroyed his B-25 on landing roll-out. On 20 September the first 31st FG Spitfires were flown into Montecorvino. Ten days later the Group's CO, Col. McCorkle, shot down an Me 210 – his first victory.

Bad weather in late September and early October reduced opportunities for aerial

Six pilots of the 308th FS standing in front of a Spitfire at Castel Volturno. Some of these men went on to become Aces on Mustangs. From the left are 1st Lieutenant Donald J Walker, Major James G Thorsen, 1st Lieutenant Hurd and Captain Leland P Molland. Kneeling are Midgett (rank unknown) and 1st Lieutenant Charles E Brown. Both Thorsen and Molland commanded the 308th FS at different times in 1944. The 'HL' code is in 20" high white letters. (C Brown)

combat as Allied ground forces pushed north up the boot of Italy, but still well south of Anzio, the location for a later invasion. The 31st FG staged into Pomigliano airfield near Naples on 14 October 1943.

Life became a mixture of violent warfare and more civilized conduct off-duty because, for the first time since February, the men were housed in permanent buildings and the Group enjoyed the use of a concrete runway from which to launch missions. The Luftwaffe sent Fw 190s to strafe the field several times a day and the poor autumn weather of rain and mud, continued to hamper Allied air operations. More interestingly, for the first time since leaving England, American women were on the scene. Donut girls handed out donuts and coffee. Nurses, Women's Army Corps girls and Red Cross girls appeared. Dances were organized and Italian families paid respects to their liberators by bringing their daughters to mix with the Group. Also, a rest camp was established on the Isle of Capri.

One of the few advantages of regular airfield-hopping behind advancing armies was finding many abandoned Axis aircraft. In their spare time mechanics and pilots would repair and test-fly these abandoned machines and compare the performance of such fighters as the Bf 109 and Macchi MC.202.

## WINTER IN ITALY

Weather permitting, the Spitfires flew ground support missions to keep the Luftwaffe away from troops, minesweeper patrols and harbour and bomb-line patrols. Some missions over Monte Cassino and Rome were flown. In November, when the 309th FS sent its full compliment of fighters on a mission, it began operating it's Spitfire Mk Vs at relatively low altitude and the Mk IXs at much higher altitude, weather permitting, so that the Mk IXs could act as top cover. On 1 November while patrolling the 5th Army bomb-line, the 31st FG engaged 15 enemy fighters and damaged two. On the 11th Pomigliano airfield was bombed and then strafed the following day. Two more enemy aircraft were shot down on the 13th in a dogfight, with Captain Virgil Fields claiming one.

A computer 'straightened' version of the 'Fargo Express' nose art (see page 41).

**Right**. Ist Lieutenant Richard Hurd , 308th FS, with his Spitfire Mk VIII at Castel Volturno, Italy, January 1944. Note the over-spray of red at the base of each propeller blade and the general dullness of the red – no white base coats and masking here! (W Skinner)

**Below**. 2nd Lieutenant William Skinner's crew chief and armourer sit on the wing of their aircraft, 'Lonesome Polecat' at Castel Volturno, April 1944. This Spitfire Mk VIII exhibits a faded *Dark Earth and Mid stone* camouflage scheme, the same as 'Fargo Express' on page 41. Note the field repainted Spitfire Mk V in the background, beneath 'Lonesome Polecat's' spinner. (W Skinner)

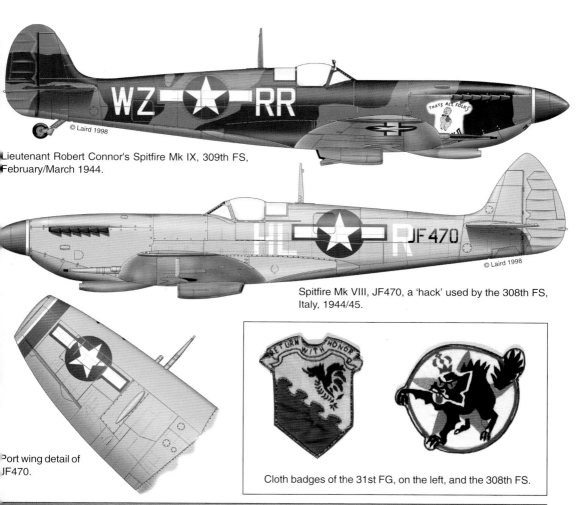

© Laird 1998

Lieutenant Robert Connor's Spitfire Mk IX, 309th FS,
February/March 1944.

© Laird 1998

Spitfire Mk VIII, JF470, a 'hack' used by the 308th FS,
Italy, 1944/45.

Port wing detail of
JF470.

Cloth badges of the 31st FG, on the left, and the 308th FS.

Spitfire Mk VIII and P-51B Mustang at Castel Volturno, March 1944. Note the Mustang's
brighter red spinner. (W Skinner)

Lieutenant Robert Connor of the 309th FS accepted his nickname 'Porky' and had it painted on his Spitfire Mk IXc shown here. This aircraft, 'Porky II', was Connor's second Spitfire. Cartoon character Porky Pig's famous line, 'that's all folks' completes the personal insignia.

Groups of letters, such as those on 'Porky II' appear under the nose of many 31st FG Spitfires in the MTO and were probably there to aid ground crews marshalling and working on the aircraft. (Connor)

Lieutenant R J Connor of the 309th FS poses for a publicity photograph in December 1943. He is standing in the cockpit of this Spitfire, a late production Mk Vc (trop) named Steve, with six stack exhaust. His crew chief, Sergeant W A Ponder, looks on. Note the two dark upper surface camouflage colours and very light shade on the tropical filter visible under the engine; the crudely painted bars added to the USAAF cocarde and the 'shadow' of the overpainted yellow ring around the star. (USAAF)

As winter continued in December the weather curtailed air activity even further. The 309th FS destroyed six enemy aircraft in the Cassino area when on bomb-line patrol on 7 December and led the Group with 47 kills by mid-December, 1943. As a Group the 31st had a total score of 119 destroyed, 28 probables and 82 damaged at that time.

'Top Brass' including: Generals Henry H 'Hap' Arnold and Carl A 'Tooey' Spaatz, Colonels Hawkins and Dean visited the Group following conferences in Cairo and Teheran. General Arnold asked a pilot he decorated with the DFC what he thought of the Spitfire. 'I think it's the finest fighter-plane ever made, General.' The Group Historian remarked on paper 'that will be censored, I'll warrant'.

## 1944 – THE BATTLE CONTINUES

In January 1944 the weather still remained the main enemy to air operations and on the 18th the Group moved forward to Castel Volturno. The new base's steel matting-formed runway proved able to withstand the muddy winter conditions. While some Italian homes were appropriated for accommodation, they were without heating and keeping warm remained a problem.

In the air over the front line on 6 January a patrol encountered 24 to 30 enemy, downing two. A bomb-line patrol on the 16th encountered 24 Fw 190s and Bf 109s and the Group downed two of them. On 20 January, 25-plus enemy were encountered and three were destroyed. Lt. Leland P. Molland of the 308th FS, who later became an Ace on P-51s, destroyed a Bf 109. All of Molland's first four victories over Bf 109s were gained in the Spitfire VIII. The personal insignia on his Spitfire was 'Fargo Express' (illustrated on page 41). Pilots preferred the Spitfire VIII because it had a slightly more powerful engine and increased range over the Mark IX, due to greater internal fuel capacity.

Captain Harry Barr stands in front of his 309th FS Spitfire Mk IX at Pomigliano near Naples, Italy, December 1943. The aircraft is named 'Skipper', his wife Micki's nickname. Barr wears a flying jacket bearing the insignia of the 41st FS. He may well have flown with this unit as the insignia is also painted on the nose of his Spitfire, together with his first victory marking. This aircraft wears the RAF Desert Scheme and the national markings have the red borders, promulgated in June 1943. Captain Barr and his ground crew names are painted on the white panel with a red outline beneath the windscreen. (H Barr)

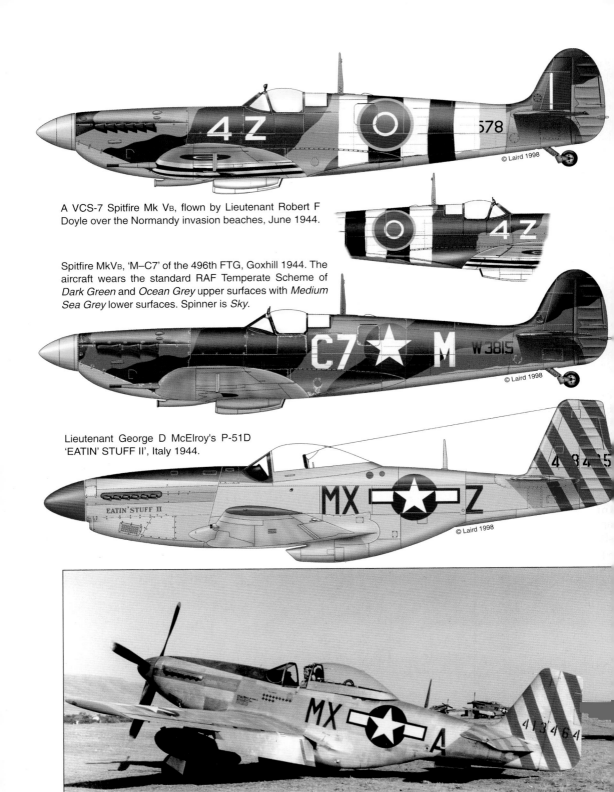

A VCS-7 Spitfire Mk V<sub>B</sub>, flown by Lieutenant Robert F Doyle over the Normandy invasion beaches, June 1944.

Spitfire MkV<sub>B</sub>, 'M–C7' of the 496th FTG, Goxhill 1944. The aircraft wears the standard RAF Temperate Scheme of *Dark Green* and *Ocean Grey* upper surfaces with *Medium Sea Grey* lower surfaces. Spinner is *Sky*.

Lieutenant George D McElroy's P-51D 'EATIN' STUFF II', Italy 1944.

© Laird 1998

P-51D Mustang 'MX-A' flown by Major Sam Brown, Commanding Officer of the 307th FS, Italy 1944/5.

## ANZIO - NETTUNO

The now famous landings at Anzio took place on 22 January 1944. On the 28th the ground echelon of 190 men went to Naples to board an LST to be transported to an airstrip at Nettuno, close to the action at Anzio. On the same day the Group put up a full force of Spitfires over Anzio and encountered many enemy aircraft, with Major Virgil Fields, C.O. of the 307th FS, getting one of them. 1st Lt. Richard Hurd downed two on the 20th and 22nd of February.

The small force of 31st FG Spitfires and men at Nettuno began hunkering down under exchanges of fire from British and German artillery and were subjected to strafing attacks from 29 January to 25 February, 1944.

Colonel McCorkle achieved his fifth victory, a Bf 109, on 6 February to become an Ace. Unfortunately Major Fields was killed the same day and so Major Alvan C. Gillem II took command of the 307th FS. The weather had been good that day and eight Spitfires were scrambled to intercept 30 enemy aircraft approaching Anzio. A Bf 109 pilot shot down Fields and pilots of the squadron achieved two kills of their own. Back on the ground everyone was stunned by the loss of Major Fields who was so well liked. Major Gillem, in his report, stated that Fields 'had recently been selected by the Group as the outstanding pilot of the 31st for a magazine article on fighter pilots in this theatre'. On the 17th the men of

**Above** and **below**. Two photos showing 307th FS Spitfire Mk Vc (trop) JK707, shot down by 'friendly fire' over the Salerno beachhead in September 1943.

Three victory markings, a 307th FS badge and the pilots name, Lt. Pryblo, are inscribed beneath the windscreen. The aircraft wears cocardes of 45" nominal diameter plus 3" yellow borders on it's upper wing and 30" plus 2" yellow border on the fuselage. (USAAF)

Lieutenant Dave McMillan, on the left, and Lieutenant Chas Souch at Pomigliano, which had a permanent paved runway, November 1943. Behind them is Spitfire Mk IXc, coded 'WZ-OO', on which the red wing tip stripes worn by 309th FS aircraft by late 1943 are visible. (J Fawcett)

the 31st FG noted in reports the anniversary of their hair-breadth escape from Thelepte the previous year.

While being close to the action enabled the short-range Spitfires to mount satisfactory standing patrols over the Anzio beachhead; the Nettuno airstrip was far too exposed as the destruction of more than a dozen Spitfires on the ground dramatically illustrated. Wisely, Nettuno was evacuated and all Spitfires were relocated further south to Castel Volturno.

A big dogfight on 18 March resulted in more victories. Four 307th FS pilots got one each and three 308th pilots downed two, bringing total 'kills' for the 308th FS to 58. With the Luftwaffe still active the 31st FG Spitfires were in combat regularly for the rest of the month. Four enemy aircraft were shot down on 21 March by the 308th FS, Hurd getting two. These and other combats on the 19th, 20th, 21st and 22nd raised the Group's enemy-destroyed total to 185.

Lieutenant Howard Baetjer of the 309th FS, beside his Spitfire Mk IX, early 1944. Note the *Insignia Red* surround to the cocarde on this Temperate Scheme Spitfire. The data-block names beneath his own are his ground crew, Sergeant Mike Mika, Corpora W F Just and Private First Class Jim Varrow. (Connor)

## GREEN AND GREY CAMOUFLAGE RETURNS

From December 1943 new replacement Spitfire Mk IXs were delivered in the RAF Temperate Scheme while Mk VIIIs still arrived in the Desert Scheme. A sizeable number of colour photos were taken, by Lieutenant William Skinner, of 308th FS Spitfire Mk VIIIs, in early 1944. This has led some authors to report that all USAAF Spitfires in the MTO wore Desert camouflage, until they were replaced by Mustangs. However the 307th and 309th received many new Mk IXs in Italy while the 308th continued to receive Mk VIIIs. The replacement Mk IXs were now in Temperate camouflage as the photos in this book testify.

## NATIONAL INSIGNIA

With the transition to star-and-bar national markings, the 31st FG Spitfires showed a wide variety of applications of the new white bars in July 1943. Some aircraft never received the red borders specified on 28 June 1943 (see appendix 1), while others retained the red borders and never received the blue ones specified on 14 August 1943. Although sizes varied, national insignia were generally 30" nominal diameter, in all four positions by April 1944, when the Group transitioned to the P-51B Mustang.

## THEATRE AND GROUP MARKINGS IN ITALY

Within the 31st FG wing tip bands were adopted as Squadron-within-Group markings and appear to have been promulgated purely at Group level. The 307th FS had no band, the 308th yellow and the 309th red. In Italy all fighters in the MTO retained their red spinners. While white codes became more uniform in size within each squadron, they still varied from 20" to 24" high.

**Right**. Major Virgil C Fields Jr. Commanding Officer of the 307th FS at Anzio-Nettuno, checks one of the replacement Spitfire Mk VIIIs received after the squadron had twelve Spitfires destroyed on the ground, by shellfire at the Nettuno beachhead airstrip during it's two months there. This machine has yet to be re-marked with USAAF insignia and wears the RAF Desert Scheme. Note the red doped fabric covering the gun ports. (USAAF

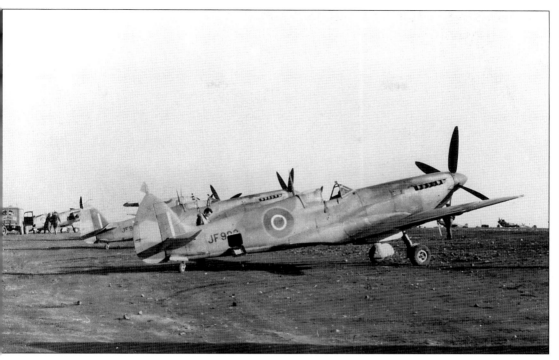

**Above**. More than a dozen 307th FS Spitfires were destroyed at Nettuno airfield and RAF marked replacements were flown in. Here a group of replacement Spitfire Mk VIIIs, all wearing Desert Scheme camouflage, await collection by 307th FS pilots. (Hagins)

**Above**. Lieutenant Robert Belmont of the 309th FS glances toward the camera while standing next to his Spitfire Mk IXc 'Thurla Mae III' in February 1944. This aircraft wears the RAF Temperate Land Scheme and has 34" high fuselage cocardes. One difference between 'Thurla Mae III' and 'Lady Ellen III' (see page 54) is the manner in which the old RAF fuselage roundel has been painted out. A minimum of fresh Ocean Grey has been used to obliterate the upper portion of the roundel, rather than the whole forward spine being painted with a lighter grey as with 'Lady Ellen III'. Note Belmont's two 'kill' markings, the crew data block visible under the windscreen and the 22" high white codes. (J Fawcett)

**Above**. 307th FS Spitfire Mk VIII and Mk IXs lined up on the road leading to Castel Volturno, Italy, March 1944. The Spitfires are about to be exchanged for P-51Bs and the whole 31st FG reassigned from the 12th AF to the 15th AF. The three aircraft nearest the camera wear the RAF Temperate Land Scheme (*Dark Green* and *Ocean Grey* upper surfaces and *Medium Sea Grey* lower surfaces), while the fourth aircraft has the Desert Scheme. (Hagins)

**Left**. J J Morris of the 308th FS, on the right, assists another ground crew member in covering a Spitfire Mk IX's canopy, which prevented any damage to the highly polished and easily scratched perspex. This photo was taken at Castel Volturno in December 1943. (J J Morris)

**Right**. Captain Leland P Molland on the left, with Major James G Thorsen at San Severo April/May 1944. Major Thorsen wears a flying jacket decorated with the 308th FS Squadron badge. He was later killed bailing out of a P-51 when his parachute failed. (Levy)

# 'LADY ELLEN III'

These four photos depict Lieutenant John Fawcett's Spitfire Mk IX 'Lady Ellen III' of the 309th FS, Castel Volturno, Italy, early 1944.

MH894 was delivered new to the 309th FS in January 1944 in the RAF Temperate Day Scheme of *Dark Green* and *Ocean Grey* upper surfaces with *Medium Sea Grey* lower surfaces. (John Fawcett's recollection of this aircraft was that it was painted shades of grey as distinct from the sandy brown colours of the RAF Desert scheme).

MH894's fuselage star-and-bars are 34" overall height and centred over the factory applied 36" RAF roundels. The 34" upper wing star-and-bars are also centred over the old RAF markings, with the upper surface camouflage pattern carefully restored using green and grey paint, rather than just one colour. Star-and-bars in all four positions carry an *Insignia Red* border, which should have been discontinued in August 1943, when *Insignia Blue* officially replaced it. For some reason the 307th and 308th FS complied with the *Insignia Blue* directive, but the 309th retained red until the squadron received Mustangs. The spinner is red with a white backing plate.

John Fawcett's recollections of fighting in Italy included the way mud got everywhere. He remembered looping a Spitfire and having mud fall from the 'floor' at the top of the loop. No matter how they tried, both air and ground crew just could never keep their aircraft clean.

The aircraft was named for Fawcett's wife and, like others in the 31st FG, had two repeated code letters, ie 'JJ' to distinguish it from another, older aircraft in the same squadron, coded 'J'.

'Lady Ellen III' on March 30 1944, the day the 309th FS officially exchanged it's Spitfires for Mustangs. (J Fawcett)

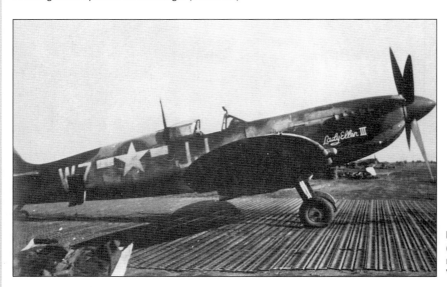

MH894 sits on the PSP (pierced steel planking) runway at Castel Volturno. (J Fawcett)

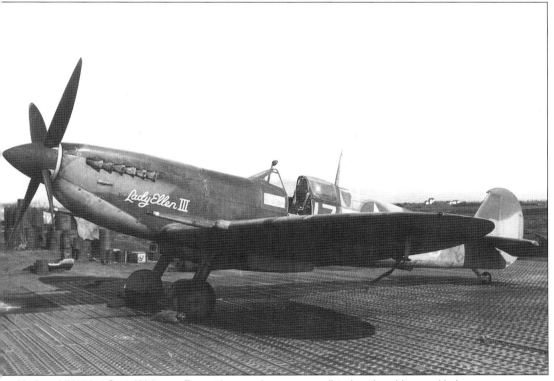

and **below**. MH894 at Castel Volturno. Fawcett's ground crew names, listed on the white panel below
[win]d screen, are Staff Sergeant Ken Benson, Sergeant 'Gable' Salerno and Corporal Jack Frost. Note that
[chan]ging the RAF roundels to star-and-bars the fuselage spine paint above the insignia has been restored in
[a lighter] colour. Also, the serial number has been painted out on the rear fuselage and reapplied in 1" high letters
[on the fi]n tip. The white code letters 'WZ-JJ' scale out to 22" high. (Fawcett)

# NEW MUSTANGS - OLD SPITFIRES

On 8 March 1944 the 31st FG heard, via rumours, that it would transition to new North American P-51B Mustangs. Although never having flown Mustangs, the Group's War Diary recorded,

> 'Although pilots think that the P-51 is the best American fighter, they think the Spitfire VIII is the best fighter in the air'.

The pilots had witnessed combat operations by the Allison engined A-36 Mustangs and were unaware of the superior capabilities of the new, Rolls-Royce Merlin engined, P-51B – so for some a surprise was in store. On 10 March two pilots were flown to Algiers to ferry the 31st FG's first Mustangs back to Castel Volturno and, the following day, Colonel McCorkle and another pilot brought two more onto base. Colonel McCorkle took a Mustang up on 14 March to test it's capabilities in a mock dog-fight against a Spitfire – the Spitfire winning because of its tighter turning circle.

Mount Vesuvius, 20 miles from the airfield, emitted a huge cloud of black smoke on the 24th. That day a pilot from the 354th FS, one of the original American manned RAF Eagle Squadrons, arrived from England to instruct on the P-51B and to overcome the pilot's reticence about their new aircraft. Five more P-51Bs, some camouflaged and some in bare metal finish, were ferried in from Bizerte, Tunisia, on the 25th with the 31st FG standing down from operations from the 28th in order to train on the P-51s. The Spitfire's swan-song was a 36-ship mission, led by Colonel McCorke over Rome, on 29 March 1944.

In March 1944 the 309th FS's first P-51B arrived at Castel Volturno and was appropriately dubbed 'First Of The Few'. The white '+' beneath the canopy indicates this P-51B was fitted with an additional 85-gallon fuselage fuel tank, post production. This marking, in black on bare-metal aircraft, also applied to P-38s and P-47s (for P-47s it indicated a modification to carry drop-tanks). The idea being that a crew chief would know that the machine was fitted with the extra tanks, without having to refer to a log-book or sign-board. Dave Wilhelm is on the far left, Ralph McCubbin leans on the propeller and John Fawcett is centre. (J Fawcett)

A sad day for the 309th FS. A line-up of their Spitfires the day they were exchanged for P-51B Mustangs. Most of these aircraft exhibit fairly clean factory applied RAF Temperate Schemes, although the nearest aircraft, an early production Mk IXc, exhibits a very faded Desert Scheme. 'VV' was flown by the squadron commander and its red wing tip stripes are clearly visible. 'XX' and 'RR' are named 'Gaye' and 'Janice' respectively. Note the light grey forward spines of 'JJ, Lady Ellen III', 'CC' and 'XX'. The new Mustangs, facing the Spitfires, exhibit two different paint schemes: Olive Drab upper surfaces with Neutral Grey under surfaces, or natural metal overall with Olive Drab anti-glare panels. (J Fawcett)

P-51B Mustangs of the 31st FG taxi in single file for a 36 'plane take off. Note the toned down national markings. These are 308th FS machines. (Mandli)

A P-51B Mustang of the 307th FS at San Severo, Italy, July 1944. This natural metal P-51B, serial 37099 coded 'MX-V', has the 31st FG red spinner and striped tail, red and yellow wing tips and yellow mid-wing Mustang recognition stripes. (Tarrant)

P-51B 'MX-A' of the 307th FS. With the change to a strategic long-range escort role, drop tanks were a common sight on 31st FG Mustangs. (via Ludwig)

Colonel Charles M McCorkle, Commanding Officer of the 31st FG when it received Mustangs in March 1944. McCorkle, a West Point graduate, was bought in to undertake a disciplined and swift transition to the new long-range Mustangs. He sits in the cockpit of his natural metal P-51B 'Betty Jane'. It's code letters, his initials CM-M, were an RAF practice carried over from the Group's Spitfire days. (USAAF)

Standing beside Colonel William A Daniel's P-51D 'HL-H' 'Tempus Fugit' at San Severo in April 1945 are the 31st FG squadron Commanders. From the left, Lieutenant Colonel James G Thorsen – 308th FS; Major Simon H Johnson Jr – 309th FS; Major Edmund M Antonini – 307th FS. In front are Colonel Daniel and Lieutenant Fred L Stoffel, the Groups Executive Officer. (Tarrant)

Lieutenant William J Skinner who flew with the 308th FS said, 'the pilots in my squadron weren't too happy about giving up the Spits for '51s. They were used to the Spit and knew what it could do. It had excellent manœuvrability, rate of climb and no restrictions on manœuvres performed. The British never gave us any flight manuals, just word of mouth. We'd ask these guys what we could or couldn't do and they'd say, "Hell, you've got a fighter plane; you can do anything you want... straight down full throttle, put your feet on the rudder pedals and pull back as hard as he can. Nothing is going to happen." You couldn't do that with many other airplanes! The Spitfire was a fun plane to fly, there was nothing to worry about. It looked nice, it flew nice too and it didn't take long before you felt very comfortable in it.'

However the Spitfire was short ranged, even with a 90-gallon drop tank. It was good for escorting tactical medium bombers, such as A-20's, B-25's and B-26's, but didn't have the range to escort the long-range strategic heavy bombers – and that was to be the Group's new role.

Colonel William A Daniel's P-51D 'HL-H' 'Tempus Fugit'. (via H Long)

## LONG-RANGE ESCORT

On 1 April 1944 the Group was transferred from tactical missions at Castel Volturno, under XII Air Support Command, to the strategic 15th Air Force and a base at San Severo, Italy. There it joined three other fighter groups as the 306th Fighter Wing, commanded by Brigadier General Dean Strother. The 31st FG was now a long-range fighter escort group.

General Arnold created the 15th Air Force in October 1943, after months of deliberation and planning. By that time the Allies in the MTO had liberated North Africa and Sicily and Allied armies were fighting the Axis on the Italian mainland. Arnold knew that the excellent air bases in and around Foggia would soon be captured and available to operate B-17 and B-24 heavy bombers able to fly the round trip to Germany. However, for the 15th AF to fulfil its purpose of attacking Germany from bases in Italy, it needed long-range escort fighters, not the range restricted Spitfire.

## MUSTANG OPERATIONS

Within two weeks of the changeover the 31st FG undertook a practice mission to the 'toe' of Italy. There was little time to spare before the 31st would be required to take it's share of the work load escorting 15th AF bombers over enemy held territory. It was a case of gaining Mustang experience 'on the job', with the first true combat mission being flown on 16 April 1944. Fifty-two 31st FG P-51B Mustangs took off to escort B-17s and B-24s to bomb locomotive repair shops at Turnul Severin – a 400 mile trip to Rumania, which was in marked contrast to the brief Spitfire missions. One Mustang was shot down by a B-24 in a 'friendly fire' incident.

This Spitfire Mk VIII, JF470, was kept as a squadron hack by the 308th FS. Note its clipped wings with red and yellow striped tips. Its colour scheme appears to be light grey upper surfaces and the original *Azure Blue* lower surfaces. Note the internal rear-view mirror. (A Bleiler)

1st Lieutenant George D McElroy, of the 307th FS, relaxes on the wing of his P-51D Mustang 'EATIN' STUFF II' at San Severo, Italy. He finished the war with four aerial victories. Both photos on this page were taken by Fred Luzzi, McElroy's armourer. (F Luzzi)

**Below**. 1st Lieutenant George D McElroy's P-51D 'EATIN' STUFF II' at San Severo, Italy, 1944/45.

Major Sam Brown crouches on the wing of his Mustang with his parachute pack. He finished the War with 15 ½ victories. Note how this aircraft's anti-glare panel is already showing signs of fading. (USAAF)

Squadrons of the 31st FG kept a number of Spitfires as 'hacks' after transitioning to the P-51B Mustang. This silver painted Spitfire Mk VIII was used by the 307th FS in 1944, with the red tail stripes of it's new Mustangs. Note the 'toned down' white areas of the fuselage star-and-bar. (Toman)

On the 21st 48 Mustangs escorted B-17s and B-24s to the oil refineries at Ploseti, one of the most dangerous targets in Occupied Europe and a 580 mile round trip. Sixty-plus enemy aircraft were sighted and 15 were claimed destroyed, three by Lt. John Ainley of the 309th FS. He became an ace that day having downed four in Spitfire Mk IX's earlier in the war. The 31st FG received an Outstanding Performance Citation from the 15th AF for it's efforts that day. By the end of the month the Group had escorted raids as far as the Messerschmitt factory near Vienna and targets at Sofia, Bulgaria; Toulon, France; and Northern Italy. Another 20 long distance bomber escort missions were to follow in May 1944.

By now the pilots misgivings about relinquishing their Spitfires were dissipating. Though opportunity for air-to air combat was decreasing in many war sectors, the Luftwaffe was extremely active over the Third Reich as many Luftwaffe Fighter Gruppen were committed to stopping the American strategic daylight bombing campaign crashing like a tidal wave over their heads from bases in England and Italy. The 31st FG pilots now knew, that on every mission over any vital German asset, they were sure to see combat.

The Spitfires usefulness to the USAAF was over. The Merlin-engined Mustang reigned supreme in the escort role and only a few Spitfire 'hacks' remained with the 31st FG to wear the new Mustang colour schemes.

A flight of 308th FS P-51Ds including 41311 'HL-C' 'Okaye' flown by Captain Leland P Molland with 11 victory markings. All these aircraft are natural metal with red noses and tail stripes. Wingtips are red and yellow and inner wing bands are the yellow P-51 'type' recognition markings. Anti glare panels are Olive Drab. (Tarrant)

# THE 496TH FIGHTER TRAINING GROUP

A little-known USAAF operator of Spitfires was the 496th Fighter Training Group (FTG). It was based at Goxhill RAF station from December 1943, before moving to Halesworth in February 1944 and remained there until the end of the war. The training squadrons within the 496th operated P-38s, P-47s, P-51s as well as Spitfires.

Spitfire Mk VA 'M–C7' serial W3815, pictured here, was one of these training aircraft. It was originally an RAF presentation aircraft named 'Sierre Leone II' and served with 611, 64 and 332 Squadrons RAF. It suffered several training accidents and was repaired before passing to the 496th FTG, who in turn passed it on to 59 OTU, RAF, on 23 March 1945.

The 496th FTG also operated target-towing aircraft as part of its training programme for new fighter pilots.

**Above** and **below**. A worn aircraft, Spitfire Mk VA W3815 of the 496th Fighter Group USAAF at Goxhill, 1944. The aircraft wears the standard RAF temperate scheme of *Dark Green* and *Ocean Grey* upper surfaces with *Medium Sea Grey* lower surfaces. It has clipped wing tips and no yellow wing leading edge strips. Spinner is *Sky*. (P H T Green)

# U.S. NAVY SPITFIRES - VCS-7

Participating in the D–Day landings in Normandy on 6 June 1944 were some of the biggest battleships of the U.S. Navy. Their gunfire pounded the German defences and spotting targets for the big guns were U.S. Navy pilots flying the older Spitfire Mk Vs.

Early in April 1944 the U.S. Navy ships were in Glasgow, Scotland with their observation float planes, the Curtiss SOC Seagull biplanes and Vought OS2U Kingfishers. Normally these aircraft were catapulted from their mother ships as gun spotters. However, it was envisaged that over Normandy such slow spotter planes would be heavily opposed and prove too vulnerable when faced with any Luftwaffe opposition.

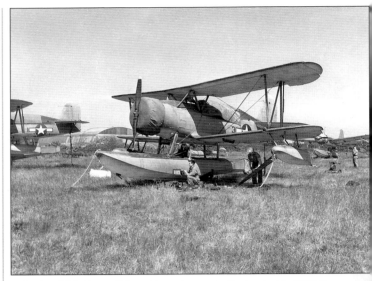

A Curtiss SOC 'Seagull' in outdoor storage in England while VCS-7 operated Spitfires over Normandy. Note the Vought OS2U Kingfisher in the right background. (National Archives)

Lieutenant Francis A Cahill prepares for another sortie over Normandy in this Spitfire Mk V '4X'.
Note the late style six-stack exhaust and roughly applied invasion stripes. (National Archives)

Lieutenant Commander William Denton Jr. United States Navy, Commanding Officer of VCS-7. This Spitfire Mk VB has a six-stack exhaust and a Rotol propeller, easily identified because it maintains its blade width right to the spinner. (National Archives)

US Navy maintenance crewmen pose with '4Q' which exhibits one kill marking. From the left are James O'Connor; C N Pfanestiel; V G Disa, ACMM; R P Theirauld, AMM3c; and Edmund Pachgio. '4Q' has the standard three-stack exhaust and early style, external armour, windscreen. (National Archives)

A plan was formulated to train all U.S. Navy spotter pilots on Spitfires and all existing spotter aircraft were flown ashore in April to be stored at Ipswich, either in hangars or under tarpaulins in the open. Pilots from six ships were gathered and formed into a new temporary squadron designated VCS-7 and commanded by Lieutenant Commander William Denton, Jr, from the USS Quincy.

Training on Spitfire Mk VB's at Middle Wallop was given by pilots of the USAAF 15th Tactical Reconnaissance Squadron of the 67th Tactical Reconnaissance Group. Because the Spitfire was an unfamiliar aircraft to Navy ground staff, the maintenance work was done with the assistance of civilian help. After training, the Navy pilots and their Spitfires were transferred to Royal Naval Air Station Lee-on-Solent. There they were placed under the command of the Third Naval Fighter Wing of the Royal Navy's Fleet Air Arm (FAA), to participate in spotting with two RAF and four FAA squadrons.

Up before dawn on D-Day the Navy pilots flew in pairs over the invasion beaches completing 34 sorties for the bombardment ships. Only one VCS-7 pilot went missing in action and he found his way home several days after the invasion. VCS-7 daily schedule of sorties began to decrease in frequency after D–Day–plus–four and VCS-7 was disbanded on 26 June 1944. One pilot flew 17 sorties during his short spotting tour of duty.

**Above** and **Below**. Lieutenant Robert W Calard poses beside his Spitfire Mk V '4R' and Ensign Robert J Adams beside '4X' in June 1944. Ensign Adams was the first American naval aviator to land in France after the invasion.

Compare the difference between the roughly painted black and white invasion stripes on these two machines. (National Archives)

## CAMOUFLAGE AND MARKINGS

The Spitfires provided to VCS-7 were a mixed bag of refurbished Mk VBs, some with the six-stack exhausts fitted from new to late production Mk Vs. Camouflage was reportedly the RAF Temperate Land Scheme of *Dark Green* and *Ocean Grey* upper surfaces with *Medium Sea Grey* lower surfaces. However, most of the photos published here – all printed from carefully chosen negatives – show far less contrast than a typical *Dark Green* and *Ocean Grey* scheme. Possibly the grey is a mixed grey to a darker shade.

Roundels were in the RAF standard six positions; 56" 'B' type, upper wings; 32" 'C' type, under wings; 36" 'C1' type, fuselage and 24" by 24" fin flashes. Code letters on both sides of the forward fuselage are white. Given the urgency with which they were applied, the black and white invasion stripes on wings and fuselage were typically roughly painted and in some cases don't even meet under the fuselage.

**Below**. Lieutenant Robert F Doyle, on the wing of his Spitfire Mk VB, shakes hands with his wingman John F Mudge. According to the official wartime caption the two had just returned from a gunfire spotting mission over the Invasion beaches in June 1944. This machine seems to wear a patched up RAF Temperate Land Scheme with the cowling grey colour lighter than the adjacent undersurfaces grey. Again, the roughly painted invasion stripes are obvious. (National Archives)

**Above**. Two pilots of VCS-7 being briefed for a mission. From the left, Wing Commander Robert J Hardiman RAF, who acted as commanding officer for all Allied Gunfire Spotting pilots; Ensign Robert J Adams, VCS-7; Major Noel East, British Army Intelligence; Lieutenant Harris Hammersmith Jr, VCS-7 and Captain John Ruscoe, Royal Artillery Gunnery Liaison Officer. (National Archives)

# Appendix 1 National Markings

## United States Army Air Forces

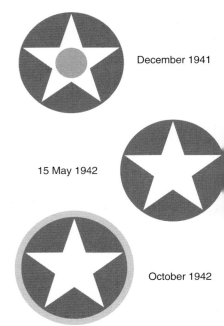

December 1941

December 1941:– Red white and blue cocarde which had been in use since 1921.

15 May 1942:– All red centre dots to be removed from aircraft in the field from this day.

15 May 1942

15 June 1942:– The 31st FG receives it's first Spitfires in England. Blue and white cocardes are to be applied in the standard four positions Officially no yellow border is to appear on any cocarde, but on some aircraft the RAF 'C1' fuselage roundels are modified to cocardes and the yellow ring remains.

October 1942:– The 8th Air Force issues orders that all aircraft under its command are to have a yellow border added to cocardes. A few 31st FG Spitfires are altered.

October 1942

November 1942:– 31st FG ground crews have the job of modifying RAF-marked Spitfire Mk V (trops) to Operation Torch markings. The result is crudely painted cocardes with yellow borders and American flag decals on the fuselage.

28 June 1943

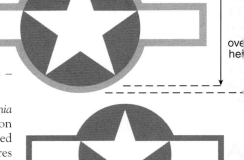

nominal diameter

ove
hei

28 June 1943:– All USAAF aircraft are ordered to add white rectangles and an *Insignia Red* border to all cocardes. Some Spitfires receive the white rectangles but no red borders – proportions varied.

14 August 1943:– *Insignia Red* borders are changed to *Insignia Blue*. Again the level of implementation varies, with the 308th FS retaining red borders until it relinquished its Spitfires in March 1944.

14 August 1943

## Royal Air Force

Throughout the period when Spitfires were provided to the 31st FG, they were delivered to the Group with factory applied RAF roundels in six positions as follows:

    32" type 'C' on both lower wings
    36" type 'C1' on fuselage sides
    56" type 'B' on both upper wings

type 'C'      type 'C1'      type 'B'

# Appendix 2 Camouflage colours and Federal Standard (FS) number equivalents

| Name | FS Equivalent |
|---|---|
| **USAAF 'ANA' (Army Navy Aircraft) Colours** | |
| No. 45, Insignia Red (Bright) | 31136, as recorded in red bordered national markings |
| No. 618, Insignia Red (Dull) | 30109-30166, **not** recorded in use on 31st FG Spitfires |
| No. 605, Insignia Blue | 35044 |
| **RAF Colours** | |
| Azure Blue | 35231 |
| Dark Green | 34096 |

| Name | FS Equivalent |
|---|---|
| Dark Earth | 30145-30188 |
| Identification Blue (Dull) | 35022-36076, no FS colour is a perfect match, 35022 is too blue |
| Identification Red (Dull) | 30109-30166 |
| Identification Yellow | 33538 |
| Medium Sea Grey | 36314 |
| Mid Stone | 30266 |
| Ocean Grey | 36152 |
| PRU Blue | 35189-35164, 35189 is too light and 35164 too grey |
| Sky | 34533-34504 |

# Appendix 3 31st FG pilots achieving four or more aerial victories flying Spitfires

| Rank and Name | Unit | victories |
|---|---|---|
| Maj. Frank A. Hill | 308th FS | 7 |
| Capt. J.D. Collinsworth | 307th FS | 6 |
| 1st Lt. Richard F. Hurd | 308th FS | 6 |
| Maj. Virgil C. Fields, Jr. | 307th FS | 5 |
| 1st Lt. Charles R. Fischette | 307th FS | 5 |
| Col. C.M. McCorkle | Group C.O. | 5 |
| Capt. Carl W. Payne | 309th FS | 5 |
| Lt. Col. Harrison Thyng | 309th FS | 5 |
| 1st Lt. John H. White | 307th FS | 5 |
| Capt. Leland P. Molland | 308th FS | 4 |
| Maj. Dale E. Shafer, Jr. | 309th FS | 4 |

# Appendix 4 Selected Bibliography

Spitfire the History, by Eric B Morgan and Edward Shacklady, Key Publishing, England

US Air Force Colours 1942-1945 European and Mediterranean Theatres of War, by Dana Bell, Arms and Armour Press, England. Also published by Squadron Signal in the USA.

Spitfire – The Story of a Famous Fighter, by Bruce Robertson, Harleyford Publications, England.

Naval Video Time Capsules, part eight – The great Armada – Operation Torch, by Roland Smith. This excellent Video is available from Roland Smith, Beck House, Escrick, North Yorks YO4 6J8, England. It includes various pieces of official Royal Navy movie footage

Spitfire the Canadians, by Robert Bracken, Boston Mills Press, Canada.

# Appendix 5 RAF camouflage - Basis and origins, as applied to USAAF Spitfires

When Supermarine Spitfires were supplied to the various USAAF units operating them, the aircraft came from the same stocks which supplied RAF squadrons .

In the spring of 1941 RAF Spitfire squadrons began confronting the Luftwaffe over the western seaboard of Europe and the *Dark Green* and *Dark Earth* upper surfaces with *Sky* lower surfaces camouflage of the early-war period proved ineffectual over the English Channel. A new camouflage scheme was developed for the ETO; a disruptive pattern of *Dark Green* and *Ocean Grey* upper surfaces with *Medium Sea Grey* lower surfaces. This was known as the Temperate Land Scheme.

The new colours officially came into effect on 11 August 1941 and were always to be applied to new-build aircraft in the same pattern. Supermarine factories used a system of flexible mats draped over the airframe as a form of masking to achieve the consistent camouflage pattern required. See figures 1, 3 and 4. As far as the authors have ascertained, all Spitfire Mk Vs supplied to the 31st FG in England from June 1942 onwards were *Dark Green/ Ocean Grey/ Medium Sea Grey* aircraft.

When the 31st FG was posted to North Africa it collected Spitfire Mk V (trop) aircraft in Gibraltar before moving on to participate in Operation Torch. These Spitfires were in the standard RAF *Desert Scheme* of *Dark Earth* and Mid-Stone upper surfaces and *Azure Blue* lower surfaces. On the production lines in England the *Dark Earth* replaced *Ocean Grey* and the *Mid Stone* replaced the *Dark Green* (figure 2). From black and white photographs the two different colour schemes are easily discerned because the *Ocean Grey* is the lighter of the two upper surface colours in the Temperate Land Scheme and the *Dark Earth* which replaced it in the Desert Scheme is the darker of the two upper surface colours in that scheme.

As the Allies advanced into Sicily and Italy, in England new-build Spitfire Mk IXs for the MTO were now being finished in the Green/Grey Temperate Land Scheme. Some of these aircraft were issued to the 31st FG. By the time the Group relinquished it's Spitfires in March 1944 a large proportion of 307th FS and 309th FS Spitfire Mk IXs were in the Temperate Land Scheme. The 308th FS standardised on Mk VIIIs which continued to be supplied in the Desert Scheme.

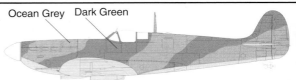

**Figure 1**. Port side of a Spitfire Mk V<small>B</small> in the *Dark Green, Ocean Grey* and *Medium Sea Grey* Temperate Land Scheme.

**Figure 2**. Port side of a Spitfire Mk Vc (trop) in the *Dark Earth, Mid Stone* and *Azure Blue* Desert Scheme.

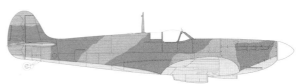

**Figure 3**. Starboard side of a Spitfire Mk V<small>B</small> in the *Dark Green, Ocean Grey* and *Medium Sea Grey* Temperate Land Scheme.

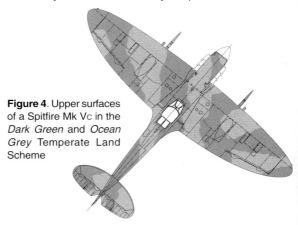

**Figure 4**. Upper surfaces of a Spitfire Mk Vc in the *Dark Green* and *Ocean Grey* Temperate Land Scheme

**Figure 5**. Port side of a Spitfire Mk V<small>A</small> in the 'B' mirror image version of the Dark Green and Dark Earth camouflage scheme which was dropped as from 14 January 1941. When the new *Dark Green* and *Ocean Grey* scheme was introduced on 16 August 1941, aircraft in the field were repainted as soon as operations permitted. This meant that some cases existed of Temperate Land Scheme Spitfires with the 'B' mirror image pattern. The Authors have discovered no USAAF Spitfires with the 'B' pattern.